HOW TO WORK
WITH ANGRY PEOPLE
AND
OUTRAGED PUBLICS

3852 Allsborough Drive
Tucker, GA 30084

Copyright © 2001 by Noel L. Griese.

First Edition

Library of Congress Cataloging-in-Publication Data

Griese, Noel L.
    How to work with angry people and outraged publics:
a seminar guide and primer of best public relations
practices / by Noel L. Griese. -- 1st ed.
    p. cm.
    Includes bibliographical references and index.
    ISBN 0-9704975-2-0

    1. Public relations--Management--Case studies.
2. Issues management–Case studies. 3. Communication in
management–Case studies. I. Title

HD59.G75 2001   659.2
                QBI01-201406

Printed in the United States of America
October 2001

Third Printing August 2003
10 9 8 7 6 5 4

How To Work with Angry People and Outraged Publics: A Seminar Guide

and Primer of Best Practices for Public Relations Professionals

by
Noel L. Griese

ANVIL PUBLISHERS, INC.
Atlanta

BOOKS BY NOEL GRIESE

How To Manage Organizational Communication
during Crisis: A Seminar Guide

How To Work
with Angry People and Outraged Publics:
A Seminar Guide

Arthur W. Page
Publisher, Public Relations Pioneer, Patriot

New Hope: Avoiding Lung Cancer

ABOUT THE AUTHOR: Noel L. Griese has been a public relations executive in the telecommunications and petroleum industries. He has also been a newspaper editor, a journalism professor at two major universities and a U.S. Army officer. Currently an author and consultant, he resides with his family in Atlanta.

TO CONTACT THE AUTHOR: email noelgriese@aol.com

TO CONTACT THE PUBLISHER: email anvilpub@aol.com
website: www.anvilpub.com
phone: 770-938-0289
fax: 770-493-7232

Contents

Preface

This guide deals with ways to reduce outrage and anger in organizational publics, with negotiating skills useful in interpersonal dealings with angry individuals and with techniques for making risk communication more effective.

When a crisis occurs, it often generates outraged publics. Consider the 1996 crash of a ValuJet airliner in Florida's Everglades, with no survivors among the passengers or the crew. The crash of the airliner was the crisis. The angry publics left in its wake included:

• *Families of victims.* Spouses, children and parents of victims were first saddened, then angry about the loss of loved ones. They were frequently critical of ValuJet safety policies, blaming the company for their losses. The media had little trouble finding survivors willing to excoriate the airline in interviews.

• *Government regulators.* The National Transportation Safety Board, upset because some of its prior recommendations about airline safety had been ignored by the Federal Aviation Administration, used the crash as an opportunity to mount an attack on the FAA. The inspector general of the U.S. Department of Transportation was outraged that the FAA had not regulated ValuJet more strictly. She participated in a number of media interviews in which she was extremely critical of the airline, and, after resigning from her government job, wrote a book critical of the airline's safety practices.

• *Employees.* The union that represented flight attendants, which had been critical of airline safety policies before the crash, became particularly strident following it.

• *Stockholders*. Investors saw much of their equity in ValuJet eroded as the carrier's stock plunged following the accident. Stockholders made their feelings known through phone calls and letters and, in particular, through face to face contact at the company's annual meetings held after the crash. Disgruntled stockholders were the subject of many media interviews.

• *Elected officials*. At Congressional hearings into the accident, several federal elected officials were highly critical not only of ValuJet but of all U.S. airlines for failing to install cargo-hold fire warning devices a year after the crash.

• *Customers*. Following the crash, large numbers of the flying public deserted ValuJet. The flyers opted to book their travel on alternate airlines. These customers may have been angry or outraged. More likely they, were frightened.

• *The media*. The initial news coverage of the crash occurred during the crisis phase, while workers were still salvaging pieces of the airplane and parts of its ill-fated passengers and crew. This media coverage was devoted pretty much to the basic facts of the crash. After the first month or so, coverage during the ensuing 12 months was often characterized by a tone of outrage on the part of reporters. A number of reporters made no secret of their personal points of view in their reports.

All these outraged publics had to be managed by ValuJet's officers and, in particular, by the company's public relations staff. In addition, the staff had to deal with communication of risk. Following the crash, ValuJet became America's most scrutinized and regulated airline. The risk of flying in a ValuJet plane after the crash was probably less than the risk of flying on any other domestic carrier, and certainly less than the risk of traveling in an auto. The odds of being killed walking across the street or driving to work were greater than the odds of being killed on a ValuJet airliner even before the crash occurred. After the crash, as a result of increased federal scrutiny and intensified regulation, the risk of traveling on a ValuJet plane became infinitesimal. While risk of flying on ValuJet after the crash may have become negligible, the public often shies away from highly publicized risk even when the risk is infinitesimal,

I am thankful to individuals who have worked on my staff over the years for their input into this guide. Those to whom I am grateful include Jayne Brady, who became a respected press secretary at the U.S. Department of Energy in Washington; Chris

Crowley, a principal in King & Crowley or Portland, Oregon, and Seattle, Washington; and Beth Hill, who became the principal in Catalyst, a Grand Rapids, Michigan, public relations agency, before returning to her love of teaching music to children.

I'd be remiss if I didn't mention Angie Horsley, a lovely young lady who was murdered by a jilted boyfriend while on my staff. I will always remember her as a promising young professional who never had the chance to fully flower.

Finally, I wish to emphasize that this is the Beta or first edition of a book that will be published in second edition form in October 2002. Readers who would like to contribute their own anecdotal experiences in working with angry people and outraged publics—no more than 200 words per submission, please—for inclusion in that future edition are encouraged to do so. E-mail them, please, to noelgriese@aol.com. If your submission is selected for inclusion, we'll get back to you with a clearance form, so please include an e-mail or snail mail address with your submission. I look forward to hearing from you!

Sincerely,

Noel L. Griese

Atlanta, September 2001

To
my wife Kathie
ever beautiful, devoted and supportive,
and to Avery, Carolyn, Dawn, Laura,
Mary, Mark, Mitch, Nate,
Nolan and Shannon
around whom
most of my adult life has revolved

CHAPTER ONE

Working with Angry Publics: The Texaco Dilemma

For two years, oil giant Texaco, like Nero, had fiddled while a racial discrimination suit smoldered. Embers fanned to flames when a disgruntled senior executive who had been downsized leaked to plaintiffs in the lawsuit some tapes he had secretly recorded during internal meetings. The tapes at first seemed to have captured fellow executives using a racial epithet onerous to black Americans. While analysis of the evidence revealed that Texaco executives did not use the "n" word on the poor-quality tapes, there is no doubt that the tapes caught company officials discussing the destruction of evidence important to the race discrimination lawsuit.

The tapes were prime evidence in federal indictments of several Texaco executives, including the former employee who had clandestinely made the recordings. The tapes caught the executives joking about "black jellybeans" sticking to the bottom of the advancement bag. Disclosure of the tapes produced anger and outrage in the minority community. Jesse Jackson called for a boycott of Texaco by minority consumers. Headlines and editorials were critical of the company.

Within 11 days, Texaco CEO Peter Bijur apologized to the minority community and the nation, and suspended all the individuals involved in the tapes. Texaco cut off retirement benefits to those involved who had retired. The lawsuit was settled for $176.1 million. The Jackson boycott dissipated, and the media turned to other targets.

A few weeks later, in May, Texaco CEO Peter Bijur was able to face stockholders at the Texaco annual meeting and say, "the value of your shares today hit an all-time high..." and boast of the rapid strides Texaco was making after only three months in providing greater opportunities for women and minorities and increasing diversity in its workplace.

Crisis management professionals were nearly unanimous in proclaiming the case to be a great triumph of the new crisis management trend, preemptive confession followed by decisive action to correct the wrong. Sometimes referred to as the *mea culpa* approach (*mea culpa* is Latin for "my fault"), the technique has proven successful in a number of test cases.

But was the Texaco response to the public relations crisis spawned by disclosure of the tapes a great example of dealing with an outraged public? Not according to crisis management guru Gerald C. Meyers, former chief executive officer of American Motors, who has devoted his subsequent career to teaching crisis management at Carnegie-Mellon University. Author of *When It Hits the Fan: The Nine Crises of Business*, Meyers said of the Texaco case to Sydney Freedburg Jr. of *New Republic* magazine, "They did a knee-jerk, which was a mindless knee-jerk in my opinion. They fell for the public relations catechism of apologies first and think later.... They've got to grow out of this. Bijur condemned 27,000 people as bigots by falling for this knee-jerk advice." Freedburg said of Meyers, "He seems offended by the new spinelessness of the '90s," adding Meyers' closing observation, "Doesn't a company have some obligation to defend its employees?"

As for the triumphant remarks to stockholders at the annual meeting, all was not love and roses at that event. Protesters gathered in force for the meeting in Rye Brook, N.Y. Attacks came from several directions. The protesters alleged race and sex discrimination, despite the apologies and other actions Texaco had taken. Jesse Jackson, present at the meeting, demanded more minority representation in Texaco management. He was backed by the Evangelical Lutheran Church, which owned a paltry 3,200 shares of Texaco, but used that leverage to demand of Texaco by September a progress report on diversifying the board.

Protesters at the annual meeting also criticized Texaco for its environmental policies and its investments in Myanmar (formerly Burma). They accused Texaco of supporting the military dictatorship in Myanmar through its 43 percent ownership in an offshore natural gas field. CEO Bijur told the protesters Texaco would consider selling its interest in the field.

Proponents of the *mea culpa* approach to crisis public relations who hail the Texaco race relations case as a model for the rest of corporate America have failed to give much consideration to the $176.1 million legal settlement, much of which went into the pockets of the lawyer who represented the Texaco employees. That lawyer was the very same Washington attorney Texaco had enriched a few years earlier in a $50 to $200 million settlement with the residents of a neighborhood in Fairfax, Va., where Texaco admitted to polluting the neighborhood's ground water. As the old adage goes, "Fool me once, your fault; fool me twice, my fault."

So, which side are you on? Was the Texaco handling of the race relations case a model for the rest of corporate America to use in dealing with outraged publics? Or was it a bungled surrender of principles?

AFTER TEXACO:
SLAYING PROTEST IN CINCINNATI

In April 2001, a white policeman in Cincinnati, Ohio, shot and killed 19-year-old Timothy Thomas, a minority resident with a record of a few misdemeanors. Mr. Thomas turned out to be unarmed. Not only that, he was the 15th black man killed by police in the city since 1995, four of them since November 2000.

The death touched off a week of rioting, the worst seen in Cincinnati since 1968 after the Rev. Martin Luther King Jr. was assassinated.

On April 14, the governor of Ohio and mayor of Cincinnati apologized for the killing at the youth's funeral.

Ohio Gov. Bob Taft, a Republican native of Cincinnati, apologized first for the police slaying of the young man. "We are praying for you, Timothy Thomas," Taft said as he looked down at the casket. "He was pulling his life together, and his untimely death was a tragedy. We are sorry about his tragic death, and we are especially grateful to Angela Leisure (the boy's mother), who called for calm in the city, even in the face of her grief."

Cincinnati Mayor Charles Lukens said, "Please accept my apology... Let us start today to build a new Cincinnati that seriously addresses issues of justice and social justice."

The gestures were lost on a dozen peaceful protesters who had gathered outside the church where the slain youth's funeral was held. For unexplained reasons, police fired thumb-sized beanbags at the protesters, slightly injuring a 7-year-old girl.

Large numbers of protesters then joined the small group and marched toward the police department's district offices for the neighborhood. Confronted by a solid line of officers when they reached the police building, the protesters raised their arms to emphasize that they were unarmed. Calm was restored after the police chief met with religious leaders in the crowd and promised to investigate why the officers fired at the crowd.[1]

APOLOGY FOR A SPYPLANE

Even when an apology is rendered, the words may not be accepted as sincere.

The Chinese have a hierarchy of words acceptable for apologies depending on the seriousness of an infraction.

When a Chinese jet fighter tailing an American spyplane collided with the plane, resulting in the Chinese pilot being lost and the 24 members of the American crew having to make an emergency landing at the Chinese airport at Hainan, the People's Republic demanded an appropriate apology. The American apologies eventually rendered, ranging from expressions of "regret" to the word "sorry," resulted in the release of the crew after a 12-day diplomatic standoff, but few officials or citizens in the People's Republic felt the apology was sincere.

In the weekend that preceded the release, American officials had sprinkled words such as "regret" and "sorry" through talks with the Chinese. Secretary of State Colin Powell rendered the first official American apology on CBS-TV's Sunday "Face the Nation" program saying

We do acknowledge that we violated their air space, but look at the emergency circumstances the pilot was facing. And we regret that, and we've expressed sorrow for it, and we're sorry that happened. But that can't be seen as an apology accepting responsibility.

There is a widow out there and we regret that. We're sorry that her husband was lost no matter what the fault was.

In an effort to make the Powell apology acceptable to the Chinese people, Xinhua, the Chinese news agency, reported what had been said with subtle changes:

Appearing on CBS television's "Face the Nation" program Sunday, Powell said: "We do acknowledge that we violated their (China's) airspace... And we regret that. We have expressed sorrow for it. And we're sorry that happened."

The secretary also repeated his regret over the loss of a Chinese pilot in the April 1 spyplane incident. He said that "there is a widow (the wife of missing Chinese pilot Wang Wei) out there, and we regret that. We're sorry that her husband was lost."

The second apology came midway through the same week. A letter delivered to Chinese officials on the Wednesday after the television program escalated the level of apology to America being "very sorry" for the pilot's death and the landing of the American plane on Hainan without Chinese approval.

With that carefully worded compromise statement, the impasse was broken. The United States avoided the full apology demanded by China. To make the apology palatable to the Chinese people, the government-run *Beijing Morning Post* put some spin on the American note with a banner headline that said, "The United States finally apologizes!"

The wording of the apology was low on the scale of what a typical Chinese would find acceptable for an incident of the magnitude involved. Why did the government relent and release the American crew? Perhaps the government officials were worried about world opinion in the face of a bid they were making for the Olympic games. Perhaps they wanted more time to examine the equipment in the aircraft sitting at the airport on Hainan without the pressure of America demanding the release of the crew. Whatever the reasons, the Chinese released the American crew, but not the aircraft. The plane, loaded with highly sophisticated espionage equipment, only some of it destroyed, would not be handed back for some time, and when it finally was returned, it was dismembered into pieces flown to the United States in a Russian cargo plane.

The United States made it clear in its own face-saving bravado that the flights off the coast of China would resume in the near future.[2]

THE WORLD IS FULL OF ANGRY PUBLICS

How often in your life and in your career have you had to deal with an angry person? Quite often, probably. You likely have to deal now and then with an angry spouse, with an angry child, or perhaps with an angry neighbor. How about at work? Have you had to deal with an angry boss lately? An angry subordinate? An outraged fellow worker? Have you ever had to deal with an angry customer?

How about outraged groups? Have you ever had to face a neighborhood association whose members were angry about a facility your company wanted to place in their neighborhood? Have you had to face an audience of flood or tornado victims who think your agency should have responded with assistance more quickly than it did?

MINI-CASE: CHEAP OVERSEAS LABOR

Situation: A large U.S. manufacturer. wholesaler and retailer of athletic shoes and related sports gear has become the subject of intense public and media criticism at home for using cheap overseas labor. Foreign adults employed in sweatshops are being paid less than a living wage, and are frequent victims of abuse by overbearing native managers. Allegations are that the company has even been exploiting child labor, paying substandard wages to young workers desperate to help support themselves and their families. Television news shows have shown footage of females hunched over machines and children at work in foreign factories making the company's products. Poignant interviews, the answers and comments of the workers dubbed in subtitles or spoken by an interpreter, bring tears to the eyes of some viewers. Sales of the company brand are falling precipitously, and the company's stock, long a stellar performer, has been heading south.

Discussion points:

1. As director of public relations for this corporation, what actions and what communication programs do you recommend that management adopt?

Resolution: The company decides to adopt two major recommendations to deal with the situation. First, it hires former United Nations Ambassador Andrew Young to report on conditions in the company's overseas plants. Second, it launches a communications campaign to publicize its Code of Conduct for employees. The Code of Conduct is printed on cards in the native languages of workers and managers, and distributed to 100,000 contract workers in Asia. Poster-sized versions of the Code are also printed, and managers are informed that they must be posted in visible places on factory floors. Managers will be tested to be sure that they understand provisions of the Code.

Discussion Points:

1. When an organization comes under public criticism, a frequent action taken is to appoint an outside expert or a blue ribbon panel to investigate and issue an independent report. In your opinion, was the appointment of Andrew Young to conduct an investigation likely to produce an effective resolution to sweatshop charges?

2. Is the distribution of cards and posters likely to produce an end to abuse by local managers? Is the distribution likely to put an end to the public relations problems brought about by the media stories?

REVIEW QUESTIONS: TEXACO CASE

1. Was Texaco's handling of its diversity crisis as described in the text a masterful example of handling angry minority customers, or did it leave much to be desired?

2. What in your opinion could have been done better?

3. Texaco used "cascading communication" to inform its employees as the crisis unfolded. What is "cascading communication?" Does it work effectively in a large organization?

REVIEW QUESTIONS: GENERAL

1. Describe the last time you had a confrontation with an angry person or group. How long ago was it? What was the outcome?

2. Can you recall a situation where the organization for which you work had to face an angry public? What were the circumstances?

3. The Japanese government recently refused to withdraw a textbook for schoolchildren which glossed over atrocities committed by the Imperial Army during World War II. When Korea, China and other nations whose citizens had been victimized drew attention to the omissions in the textbook, Japanese officials refused to apologize for the World War II activity. The Japanese head of state further provoked the protesting nations by paying a visit to the Shinto shrine that honors Japanese soldiers who died in the war, some of them convicted war criminals. However, the same government leaders were considering a formal apology to American prisoners of war who suffered at the hands of the Japanese Army. Discuss the pros and cons of the government positions.

4. In a 2001 case, an American spy plane collided with a Chinese fighter that intercepted it. The Chinese jet crashed and the pilot was lost. The U.S. plane with 24 people on board landed on an offshore Chinese island and the American crew was detained. The Chinese government demanded an apology from the United States. To get the crew released, the U.S. government said it was "sorry," which was not an acceptable apology by Chinese standards. To compromise, the U.S. said it was "very sorry," escalating the *mea culpa* to a sort of *mea maxima culpa*. The term *mea culpa* doesn't exactly apply in this case, since the U.S. was merely saying it regretted the incident, not that it was at fault and apologizing. At any rate, was the U.S. response the appropriate one in your opinion?

5. An attack on the World Trade Center in New York City and

the Pentagon in Washington in September 2001 outraged the American people. Some of those involved in planning the attack died during it. If others who were involved but survived are found, would an apology from them be suitable? What additional actions might be appropriate?

FURTHER READING

Dougherty, Devon. *Crisis Communications: What Every Executive Needs To Know.* New York: Walker and Company, 1992.

Fearn-Banks, Kathleen. *Crisis Communications: A Casebook Approach.* Mahwah, N.J.: Lawrence Erlbaum Associates, 1996.

Griese, Noel L. *How To Manage Organization Communication during Crisis.* Atlanta: Anvil Publishers, 2001.

Karrass, Chester L. *Give & Take: The Complete Guide to Negotiating Strategies and Tactics.* New York: Thomas Y. Crowell, Publishers, 1974.

McKay, Matthew, Martha Davis and Patrick Fanning. *How To Communicate: The Ultimate Guide to Improving Your Personal and Professional Relationships.* New York: MJF Books, 1983.

Meyers, Gerald C., with John Holusha. *When It Hits the Fan: Managing the Nine Crises of Business.* New York: Mentor/New American Library, 1986.

ENDNOTES

[1] John Nolan, "Cincinnati mayor imposes curfew as violence over police shooting spreads," *Atlanta Journal-Constitution* (April 12, 2001), p. 1; Ernest Holsendolph, "Mayor tells Cincinnati he's sorry," *Atlanta Journal-Constitution* (April 15, 2001), p. 1.

[2] Associated Press, "U.S. crew heads for weekend reunion," *Atlanta Journal-Constitution,* April 12, 2001, p. 1.

CHAPTER TWO

Working with Angry Individuals

While public relations is concerned with building favorable relations with groups of people, it seems appropriate at the outset to discuss angry individuals and how to work with them. Considering the individual will prepare us to generalize information from individuals to the groups of publics with which public relations practitioners are normally concerned.

WHY ARE AMERICANS SO ANGRY?

In Alabama recently, an angry female driver who had been cut off in traffic caught up with the driver of the offending vehicle at a traffic ramp, got out of her car, walked up and shot and killed the female driver of the other auto.

An isolated example of road rage that will never be repeated? Hardly. According to the American Automobile Association's Foundation for Traffic Safety, incidents of violently aggressive driving by enraged motorists have risen seven per cent per year in the 1990s.

With each passing year, the number of Americans who feel pushed to the breaking point and then explode in uncontrollable anger is on the rise. That's why we're increasingly seeing stories in the mass media about road rage in Atlanta, about sky rage at a crowded airport or in an airplane over the heartland, or even about "sidelines rage." Sidelines rage? That's right. In Pennsylvania recently, a children's football game ended in a brawl involving more than 100 coaches, players, parents and fans.

Rage knows no boundaries. It's a little more likely in urban areas, but that doesn't mean it's absent from rural locations. It may occur in the elderly as well as the young. And lest you think it's confined to males suffering from an overabundance of testosterone, the research indicates females are as likely to fly off the handle as males, although the ladies are less likely to get physical. But even in that regard, as regular viewers of the *Jerry Springer Show* on television will attest, it's not at all out of the ordinary even for enraged *females* to get physical.

What's causing all this rage? Among the triggers, according to the experts, are (1) time, (2) technology and (3) tension.

Time. Americans work longer hours than anyone else in the world. We recently surpassed even the Japanese, the only culture where workers had been ahead of us. All those hours cut down on the quality of life we enjoy—and make us prone to anger.

Technology. Computers, cell phones, pagers and other tech devices were supposed to make our life easier. They are in fact doing just the opposite. It takes a lot of time to answer all those e-mails, or to get the information we need by surfing the net. It used to be possible to go on vacation and hide from the office. Now we're on call 24 hours a day every day! We now live in a 24/7/365 culture.

Tension. Because of the increased stress in our daily lives, we have less patience. "I'm stressed!" is a phrase we hear increasingly these days.

We live in affluent times, but these "easy" times have unfortunately brought out some of the worst traits in people. The South, once the bastion of civility, has become as uncivil as the rest of the country. Now, just about anywhere in the nation, the least inconvenience is likely to touch off a fit of rage in almost anyone.

Leslie Charles, author of *Why Is Everyone So Cranky?*, contends that never have so many people living in such abundance been so unhappy. "There are more of us than ever," he writes, "all wanting the same space, goods, services, or attention. Everyone thinks, 'Me first. I don't have time to be polite.' We've lost not only our civility but all tolerance for inconvenience."

Think about some of the daily annoyances that trigger anger in us. Computers crash, frustrating us. We get caught in traffic gridlock, due partly to more vehicles on the road, but also to more accidents caused by road rage. Telephone calls put us in endless do-loops of recordings telling us to push this button, then that one, until we get cut off and have to start all over again. All these annoyances give us the impression that we not longer control our lives and destinies. This sense of helplessness leads to rage, the experts say.

Timothy McVeigh may have been the last person alive who thought he was still the captain of his ship and master of his soul—and boy, was he wrong! It was, after all, controlled rage that got him in trouble at Oklahoma City—and led him as a convicted terrorist-murderer to the death chamber.

COOLING YOURSELF DOWN

Although whistling may be good for a boiling teapot, the experts say that venting, while it might make you feel better for a few seconds, accomplishes nothing. "Catharsis is worse than useless," says Iowa State University psychology professor Brad Bushman. His research shows that letting anger vent makes people more aggressive, not less. "The people who react by hitting, kicking, screaming and swearing just feel more angry," he says.

Temper tantrums are bad for you physically as well as psychologically. On the physical side, anger causes the body to produce hormones like adrenaline. While adrenaline and related biochemicals may have benefited Neanderthals by preparing them for flight or fight, to much of these hormones today make you vulnerable to stroke and heart attack. Learning to control outbursts of anger will have far more lasting and positive results.

If you find yourself losing your temper, here are some hints for regaining self-control.

Control your tongue and your brain. When you're angry, you're far more likely to say things you'll later regret. According to research, anger only lasts for a few seconds—unless you feed it with negative thoughts. It's your thoughts that control your anger. If an idiot cuts you off in traffic and makes you angry—forget it! Let him or her drive on out of your life. Stop thinking about catching up with the driver to return the favor or make a gesture. Grow up! Cool down!

Recognize your hot buttons. There are words and actions that can get under just about anyone's collar. Sometimes they provoke an individual past annoyance into anger. Each time you find yourself growing annoyed or angry, consciously think about what triggered the emotion. Start keeping a record or diary of these "hot buttons" today. Once you recognize them, you'll find it's a lot easier to control them when you confront them in the future.

Cut through the hot buttons to the real issues. You may think it's your mate's habit of leaving the cap off the toothpaste that gets you really angry, but chances are there's a bigger issue involved. Is the real issue a set of attitudes your parents instilled in you about cleaning your room that's really at work? After all, a cap off the toothpaste is hardly worth getting out the shotgun to do in a mate.

Avoid name-calling. Nothing is more likely to escalate an argument into rage than calling someone a name that you know presses one of the other person's hot buttons. Husbands and wives soon become expert at taunting partners into rage. The best antidote to anger is empathy—but it's hard to empathize with someone you've labeled a jerk, a slut, a slob, an idiot or something worse.

Tell yourself you choose not to be angry. Believe it or not, such affirmations work, according to the experts. If you're a person prone to fits of anger, you may have to repeat that injunction a few hundred times a day at first, but eventually, you'll find you've regained self control and have to say it less often.

Use a physical cue with your affirmation. When you say, "I choose not to be angry," do something physical at the same time. It might be something as simple as pressing your thumb to a finger or touching one hand with the other. Eventually, you'll find the physical cue calming you down even in the absence of your repeating the mental affirmation about choosing not to become angry.

COOLING DOWN THE OTHER PERSON

When you find that you have to help someone else who has lost his or her temper to cool down, a slightly different set of skills will be useful.

Stay calm. Letting your own anger loose will only make things worse. Talk quietly and slowly. Let the other person know that you understand. "I know you're angry, and in your shoes I'd be angry too."

Refuse to engage. Step back from the angry individual. Retreat. Don't advance until the other person is back in control. Don't invade the other person's emotional (and physical) space.

Find something to agree on. Look for common ground. "It's really unfortunate that this accident occurred. Do you agree that we need to call 911?"

REVIEW QUESTIONS AND EXERCISES

1. Suppose that you find yourself getting angry whenever you're on the expressway driving to and from work. The other people in your lane always seem to be driving either too fast or too slow. They rudely cut you off. More than once, you've felt an urge when someone squeezes in between you and the car ahead to accelerate and plow into the rear end of the offender. You've tried venting—yelling obscenities at the offenders—but that doesn't seem to help. What can you do to restore sanity to your life during these daily commutes?

2. A neighbor has knocked on your door. You answer it, and the neighbor angrily informs you that your dog has dug up his prize rose bush. He's really outraged. What are your first words and actions?

CHAPTER THREE

Basic Public Relations Concepts

This chapter outlines basic public relations concepts commonly used in working with angry people and upset publics.

The previous chapter discussed anger and the individual. When we talk about public relations, we're usually referring to creating good will among *groups* of individuals. This chapter and the remainder of the book deal with relations with *publics*, as opposed to relations with a single angry individual.

Let's begin by looking at a definition of public relations. Public relations, corporate communications, public affairs, public information... all are terms for people employed in the field of influencing public opinion.

There are many definitions of public relations. Most, even if memorized, are usually forgotten in a very short time. One definition that is easy to remember comes from Arthur Page, the public relations vice president of AT&T from 1927 to 1946. Page liked to say that "Public relations is 90 percent doing and 10 percent talking about it." That's a way of saying that an organization's actions are more important than what it says in creating the public's opinion of the organization's reputation.

The word "reputation" figures in many contemporary definitions of public relations. Some practitioners like to refer to themselves as engaged in reputation management. That's a part of public relations, at the top end of the spectrum where the more sophisticated part of the practice is.

At the other end of the public relations continuum, down at the bottom in stature, is press agentry. The goal of the press agent or promoter is to get publicity, good or bad, for a client. Many public relations professionals prefer to distance themselves from publicity or press agents. But in fairness, press agentry was an important part of early public relations practice, and remains a significant part of it today. Modern-day press and publicity agents are frequently engaged in promoting movies, Broadway shows and other aspects of the entertainment industry. Sometimes they work for the actual stars, sometimes for production houses. They may work for athletes and other celebrities.

In the category of "other celebrities" are individuals like Kelly Flynn, the female nuclear bomber pilot who faced court-martial for disobeying orders not to see a lover and for lying about the fact that she had. The public probably doesn't realize that behind the sympathetic media canopy raised in her defense were two Atlanta public relations professionals who had responded to a request for help from Kelly's family.

The point is, contemporary public relations people are often engaged in placing product publicity for various commodities or services. We all know the power of publicity. Before looking down your nose at the humble press agent, remember that publicity usually costs a lot less than advertising.

Between the two public relations extremes of reputation manager and press agent are various functions like investor relations, speech-writing, newsletter editing, informational video production, issues management and persuading various subsets of the general public to behave in desired ways.

PUBLIC RELATIONS AND PERSUASION

Public relations is very much about persuasion. That's not the only thing public relations is about, but it's an important part. What public relations practitioners frequently want to do is persuade people to think in certain ways or behave in certain ways that are favorable to the organization for which the practitioner works.

The audiences that the public relations practitioner seeks to persuade and influence may be employees, consumers, adversaries or any number of other groups.

Practitioner are usually more concerned about persuading various publics to hold attitudes and opinions favorable to an organization than in getting them to buy something. The practitioners work to create attitudes, beliefs, and opinions that make an audience or set of publics favorably predisposed to an institution, agency or individual. Attitudes and opinions are predispositions for people to act in certain ways. When a practitioner engages in influencing attitudes and opinions, the persuader is really aiming to get the audience to act in a certain way: to vote for a candidate, to support the corporate goals, to stop interfering with a construction project, to be predisposed to buy a product or service or take some similar action.

PUBLIC RELATIONS AND NEGOTIATION

There is a movement in public relations circles today toward studying the literature of negotiation and arbitration. Some of the leading academic thought favors a recognition that public relations professionals are more often engaged in mollification and pacification of outraged publics than with the actual task of seeking to persuade.

If you're one of the folks who subscribe to the Grunig school of thought that public relations is mostly about negotiating, remember that negotiation is based in persuasion. You can still believe in negotiation as the core of public relations without disputing that public relations is very much involved with persuasion.

THREE KINDS OF TRUTH

Most people believe there's only one kind of truth—*the* truth, *their* truth, the *one and only* thing that is true.

In reality, truth can take a lot of forms. Here are three important ones.

Empirical truth. This is the truth of the scientist, the truth of numbers, the truth of replicable experiments, the truth of equations and formulas that hold true in repetition after repetition. Empirical truth is in the domain of the scientist and engineer, although all of us deal at times in empirical truth.

Consensual truth. This is the truth of the group. The group gets together and agrees on a number of things. This is the truth of the public opinion poll or attitudinal survey.

Revealed truth. This is religious truth. It's revealed by a Supreme Being, usually to a prophet or disciples. Sometimes this category of truth may be disclosed to the general public through the intervention of a prophet or by some sort of miraculous event.

One reason a cleric arguing the literal truth of the Bible and a scientist discussing evolution will likely never agree is that the two are concerned with two completely different kinds of truth. The cleric is in the realm of revealed truth, the scientist argues from empirical fact. The two different kinds of truth may overlap, but more likely will be mutually exclusive.

CREDIBILITY AND TRUST

Those who work in the realm of persuasion need at least a passing familiarity with the concept of credibility. Credibility is a synonym for believability. Academics who do research on communication tend to prefer the term credibility for the concept.

Three types of credibility are important to communicators.

Source credibility refers to the believability of the sender of a message. Does the message come from a source that the intended receivers of the message are likely to believe?

Message credibility refers to the believability of the message itself.

Channel credibility refers to the believability of the medium used to transmit the message.

A 1996 survey of 1,100 consumers conducted by the international public relations firm Porter/Novelli found that American disbelief in institutions and leaders (source credibility) was at an all-time low.

The current disillusionment that characterizes American public opinion of government and business institutions began soon after the John F. Kennedy assassination, perhaps with the widespread public realization of government deception about the war in Vietnam. The Watergate scandal that led to the resignation of President Richard Nixon contributed to the disillusionment. Other events also contributed. Incidents like the *Exxon Valdez* and corporate reengineering and downsizing certainly played roles in the loss of respect for corporations. As for the mass media (channel credibility), people all too often realized the oversimplification of many and downright wrongness of some news reports.

For whatever reason the loss of credibility began, people who monitor public opinion were beginning to refer by 1996 to an "Age of Cynicism."

Credibility as a variable is highly correlated with trust. People who find a source to be credible or believable will also likely trust the source. The two variables are interchangable words; the concept of either plays a key role in whether an audience accepts messages from a source or is skeptical of those messages.

ATTITUDES, OPINIONS, BELIEFS (AOBS) AND VALUES

Opinions are transitory mindsets, usually on a current topic, that are not held for very long and which can usually be influenced fairly easily. We have opinions about whether or not the accused really committed the crime, about who should be elected President. We have opinions about controversial issues covered in the evening news, such as whether or not adulterous employees of the military should be discharged, or whether or not a government official is involved in immoral relationships.

Attitudes are held with more intensity and over greater periods of time than opinions. Often, parental training and values are involved in the attitudes we hold. We have attitudes about abortion, about what is right and wrong, about what is moral and immoral, about what is ethical behavior and what is unethical. These deep-seated attitudes, the result of childhood training by our parents, of role modeling and the influence of educational institutions, are powerful influencers of human behavior.

Beliefs are things we hold dear that can't be validated by empirical or consensual truth. Beliefs are usually validated by revealed truth. We believe in God. We believe that all humans are endowed with immortal souls. We believe in the literal truth of the *Bible*, the *Torah*, the *Koran*.

Values generally refer to qualities or traits that we admire and emulate. Integrity may be one of our values. Honesty might be another.

QUALITIES OF AOBS AND VALUES

Directionality. AOBs and values have directionality. We are either for something, against it, or neutral towards it. We have positive or negative feelings towards an object or person. The thing about which we have an AOB—be it inanimate or a person—in academic research is referrred to as an "attitude object."

Intensity. Attitudes, opinions, beliefs and values can be held with varying levels of intensity. The less intense the AOB or value is held, the easier to neutralize or change it.

MINI-STUDY: A CASE OF GREED?

Situation. It's 1997. Columbia/HCA, a public company that buys and operates hospitals, has become the subject of a continuing, intensive investigation by the U.S. Department of Justice. Although it isn't exactly clear what Justice is investigating, the U.S. attorneys involved seems to feel that Columbia/HCA has been charging Medicare/Medicaid patients too much, thereby cheating the government, although that's not entirely clear. As the investigation progresses, federal investigators indict three midlevel Columbia managers on Medicare fraud charges. The company's stock plunges, and shareholder lawsuits are filed, alleging that management failed to prevent the alleged malfeasance. It becomes obvious that the very survival of the corporation is at stake. In the wake of the federal investigation, 11 states launch their own investigations into billing practices at Columbia/HCA-operated hospitals. Columbia/HCA is under fire and it has had to react to the crisis.

Discussion Points

1. Based on what you've read so far, what groups or classes of people are angry or outraged at Columbia/HCA?
2. What is likely to trigger a Justice investigation of a company? Why did Justice decide to investigate Columbia/HCA?

The new management team. After the initial subpoenas were issued by the Justice Department, and it became obvious that a major crisis threatened the survival of Columbia/HCA, the company's board forced its CEO and its president to step down. The board, led by a large stockholder, installed a new management team headed by Thomas Frist, the founder of the company, who had been serving as a board member. Frist's appointment was parallel in many ways to Warren Buffet being named to head scandal-ridden Salomon Brothers in 1991. On his arrival, Buffet made crystal-clear his emphasis on ethics when he said to employees: "If you lose money for the firm by bad decisions, I will be very understanding. If you lose reputation for the firm, I will be ruthless." Frist begins reacting to the crisis with an entirely new public relations team that includes senior vice president of corporate communications Vic Campbell and international public relations firm Burson-Marsteller.

Discussion Points

1. What would motivate Warren Buffet to say he's more concerned about what employees do to affect Salomon's reputation than with whether or not they make money for the firm?

2. Is the appointment of a new management team appropriate when a company is losing public confidence?

3. Is it wise for a company being investigated by the government to cooperate fully in the investigation?

Frist's first actions upon his return to leadership. As the returning leader of Columbia/HCA, Frist spoke of the need to transform the company's culture. "I want to make changes that will clarify our company's business focus, institutionalize a corporate culture that emphasizes universal values of integrity, openness and cooperation, and enable the Columbia/HCA family of employees and affiliated physicians to provide superior care to patients," he said. He also promised to go to Washington to talk with legislators and regulators personally if he learned through his own independent investigation what (if any) laws have been broken by the company.

Frist told the *Boston Globe*, "I have to take decisive action in a responsible way, gain credit and credibility... and maybe get an audience with them as CEO. We'll go to Justice and say, 'Here's what we're going to do,' and then I've got to follow through and make sure these things are done." The company retained the Washington law firm of Latham and Watkins and accounting giant Deloitte & Touche to recommend new policies and work on government issues. It appointed Alan Yuspeh, a recognized expert on corporate ethics, to the new position of senior vice president of compliance. A new employee relations policy in which executive doors are open to employees is instituted. Frist himself tries to reach out to employees, the vast majority of whom are dismayed by the negative publicity surrounding the company.

Discussion Points

1. If Mr. Frist goes to the Department of Justice to say he's going to change things the way Justice wants, will he likely be welcomed? Will the visit likely end the investigation, or is he being naive?

2. Should an organization have an ethics officer? Who would be best qualified—someone from auditing, or perhaps the company lawyer?

3. What emotions are employees likely to be feeling as the crisis unfolds?

4. How might Columbia/HCA negotiate or arbitrate a solution with the Justice Department? With state governments?

The new president's views. The new president of Columbia/HCA, Jack Bovender Jr., said soon after assuming that role that the company "must return to its emphasis on local community services rather than trying to develop a national brand or profile."

He too was a believer in managing the reputation of the company. "The company needs to build the confidence of our publics," he stated. "Our reputation, our integrity has suffered since that first government visit at El Paso. We need to restore confidence in everyone—our employees, our patients, our investors, the public." He said, in addition, that Columbia/HCA was ready and willing to cooperate in any government investigation, and that he would work with the company's lawyers to "get a handle on what the issues are. Then, I'll help them determine what organizational changes need to be made and what systems need to be put in place to ensure that these kinds of things don't happen again."

Discusssion Points

1. How about the reputation of the organization. Is it impor-

tant? Who ought to be in charge of protecting it? If you answer "public relations should be in charge," can public relations do that job alone?

2. How do you build the confidence of various publics in an organization once the confidence has been lost?

REVIEW QUESTIONS AND EXERCISES

1. The President of the United States is suspected of having had an illicit affair with a young intern. It may be true, it may not. Who are the major constituent publics of the President? What attitudes, opinions, beliefs and values are likely to come into play among these publics to color what they think as the allegations fly?

2. You are concerned about how credible employees at your organization find pronouncements from the organization's management. How do you go about measuring credibility?

3. A scientist from the Centers for Disease Control, a rabbi and a young female college student from an affluent family have entered into a conversation on abortion. What types of truth are each likely to draw upon in the discussion? Will the three ultimately agree on a common position?

REFERENCES, RESOURCES AND SUGGESTIONS
FOR FURTHER READING

Dougherty, Devon. *Crisis Communications: What Every Executive Needs To Know.* New York: Walker and Company, 1992.

CHAPTER FOUR

The Public Relations Process

There are any number of processes which can be helpful to a professional approaching a public relations problem such as dealing with an outraged public. The Public Relations Society of America, for example, describes in the materials given to practitioners preparing to take the Society's arduous accreditation exams several processes helpful in analyzing public relations problems. Following is another such process, this one entailing eight steps. Hopefully it will prove useful to you.

Step one — Research the problem

In the first step of the process, you need to get your facts together. An immense amount of useful resource material is available to the practitioner who seeks it.

There are two academic disciplines which yield information of value to the practitioner. Most academic research falls into one of the following two categories.

• *Historiography* refers to the information brought to us through the discipline of history. Historiography is the art of analyzing historical fact to glean useful guidelines. When a practitioner reads a public relations case study for the lessons it contains, he or she is benefitting from historiography. While the case studies may be written by people from any number of academic backgrounds, such writing relies heavily on the sort of skills for which historians are noted.

• *Empiricism* refers to information brought to us by scientific researchers in the form of opinion polls, attitudinal surveys and behavioral research. Empiricism refers to collecting information that has numerical precision. For the public relations practitioner, the information collected by social scientists—sociologists, psychologists and political scientists, for example—can be beneficial in the influencing of various publics.

The two forms of academic research are not mutually exclusive. Historians often count things, and social scientists often rely on the history of prior research. Both sources of information can be helpful.

Another way of classifying research data is by the categories of formal vs. informal information. Formal data are such things as scientifically conducted polls and surveys, where statements of probability and precision can be made about results. Informal information, on the other hand, refers to data that are helpful but lack scientific precision. Going out and talking to 10 people on the street to learn how they feel about an issue or problem will lend you helpful insights, although the information may not be representative of a population, and is therefore informal rather than formal.

The amount of information available to any individual who can read, use a computer, or even watch television is growing exponentially. What data bases yield the most valuable information? To list only a few of the more valuable:

• *The PRSA Body of Knowledge.* Some of the most important information developed in the discipline exists in the Body of Knowledge assembled by the Public Relations Society of America (PRSA). The Body of Knowledge is essentially a bibliography of important knowledge that has appeared in reliable sources such as academic journals. The notations include brief descriptions of the contents of the books and articles that make up the database. The collected information is available on computer disks. Contact PRSA in New York to get a copy.

• *The world wide web.* Powerful search engines are available to help you find information on the internet. Once you're at one site identified by a search engine, hypertext links at that site can get you to other databases with related information. Some of the search engines can even find all the references made to a key word (such as the name of your organization) in chat rooms on the world wide web and internet.

• *Monitoring services.* A number of commercial services provide information on what is appearing in various information sources such as newswires, newspapers and other media. Many of these services operate online databases which can be accessed by computer for a charge.

• *Trade magazines and academic journals.* Some of the best information about current public relations practice is to be found in academic journals and for-profit newsletters and magazines.

Step two — State campaign objectives

Before you start communicating or otherwise launching a public relations campaign, you need to have an idea of what you plan to accomplish. It's a good idea to state your objectives right at the beginning of your written plan. This statement of objectives might include a listing of mission, vision and principles. Those are popular things at the moment. But in most cases, a simple enumeration of three or four things you hope to accomplish will get you started on a written plan. Unfortunately, many harried practitioners skip this part of the planning.

Step three — Identify key publics

One of the first things you need to do in approaching a public relations problem is to identify key publics. Who will you be dealing with? Key publics, stakeholders, constituent publics, call them what you will, they'll include publics internal to your organization (employees, retirees, board of directors, management, labor, dealers) and external to it (neighborhood residents, customers, vendors, industry partners, allies, general public). You can slice up the constituent publics with whom you need to communicate in any number of ways. The important thing is to try to make your listing as comprehensive as possible.

Step four — Identify key media

You might think of categorizing the media you'll use in communicating with your key publics as falling into one of four quadrants or cells. You can dichotomize the media into interpersonal vs. mass media, and into controlled media vs. uncontrolled.

• Examples of uncontrolled mass media are the news and entertainment components of radio, television, newspapers and magazines. If you put out a news release to newspapers, radio and television, you have no control of whether or not you message is used, or the way it is used. If a newspaper decides to use all or part of it as a story, it may modify the content of your message as it sees fit.

• Examples of controlled mass media include advertising you pay to place in the commercial mass media, your company newspaper or your organization's web page. In these examples, your message appears exactly as you want because you've paid for the distribution.

• Examples of controlled interpersonal channels include a telephone hot line where your employees provide information according to your scripts or a telephone hot line where you control the message communicated.

• Examples of uncontrolled interpersonal channels include rumors on the company grapevine (you can of course attempt to reduce misinformation by putting out correct facts in a controlled channel) or random conversations in internet chat rooms (search engines can help you find out what people are saying to one another in these chat rooms and at internet and world wide web sites about your organization).

Step five — Identify key messages

You need to write down the specific facts you want to communicate in any given situation. What are the "must air" sound-bites you want to get into the television interview? What are your holding position statements for the crisis facing your company? How will you work these key points into your answers to specific questions from media reporters and other publics?

After you've finished identifying your key publics, key media and key messages, you may want to do some additional research. After all, it's unlikely that the problem facing you is unique. Someone has probably faced the same problem before, and handled it well. Time to do some research to see if you can learn from others before falling over your own feet!

Step six — Plan the campaign

The next step in the process is to plan your public relations campaign or effort.

You might include at the beginning of your written public relations action plan a short description of the project for which the plan is written and a list of the key players.

The balance of the plan will be a listing of the actions you plan to take, the person(s) responsible, a date when an action is to be started and a date when the action is to be completed.

Step seven — Communicate and act

Once you've enumerated all the things you plan to do during a specific public relations project or campaign, it's time to begin implementing your plan. The plan will invariably involve taking some actions and doing some communicating.

Of the two things, actions in the public interest are far more important in determining an organization's reputation than communication. Remember what Arthur Page said? "Public relations is 90 percent doing, and 10 percent talking about it."

Check your plan to be sure that your organization's actions are something that will make you and all of the employees of the organization proud! Do that, and everything else will pretty much fall into place.

You must of course still communicate the fact that your organization is performing in the public interest. Be sure you consider using all the channels available to you—the uncontrolled mass media, the controlled mass media, uncontrolled interpersonal channels and controlled interpersonal channels.

As you complete various tasks on the Public Relations and Information Schedule, check the item off. Be sure to review the plan frequently to be sure you're not overlooking anything!

Step eight — Evaluate

The last step in the process is to evaluate the success of your campaign or project. This is where you check to see if you have accomplished the objectives you set at the start of the campaign.

The same tools you used in the first (research) step of the process are used in this step. You may wish to use formal surveys and polls, or informal indicators of success such as newsclips and logs of phone calls, to provide objective evidence of what you accomplished in the campaign. You may wish to do some historical research, or you may want to stay in the domain of the scientist with empirical evidence. Most likely, you'll use both

The evaluation stage of a campaign is usually the research part of the next step in your public relations process. That is, the public relations process is pretty much a cyclical, repetitive thing where research leads to a plan leads to communication and action which is evaluated, with the results of the evaluation starting the process all over again.

MINI-CASE: EMPLOYEE OUTRAGE
AT DELTA AIRLINES

Situation. It's May 1997. Delta Airlines Chairman Ronald Allen catches the investment world by surprise, announcing that he will retire before the end of July. But the truth is quickly published in the *Wall Street Journal*—Allen has been forced to retire by the airline's board of directors. What's unusual is that the Delta board of directors decided to dismiss Allen after he had led the company from the abyss of deep financial trouble to record profitability.

The Leadership 7.5 Plan. In 1994, Allen, with the help of management consulting firm McKinsey & Co., launched a campaign dubbed "Leadership 7.5" to cut Delta's annual operating costs by $2 billion. In July, the month Allen retired, Delta announced profits of $886 million for the fiscal year, a remarkable turnaround from the losses being posted in the early 1990s. Unfortunately, the financial turnaround was accomplished at a human cost that left Delta's employee force demoralized. Delta had enjoyed a paternalistic culture, and the company's exemplary relationship with employees had helped build a customer service base unrivaled in the airline industry. Flight attendants, mechanics and ramp crews had rejected unionization, and many employees talked of the company in terms of family. All that ended with the Leadership 7.5 restructuring of the company. The restructuring plan cut 12,000 jobs from the 69,000 employees who made up the Delta workforce. Flight attendants and employees in some other departments were told they'd have to take pay cuts as well as reductions in vacation time and health benefits.

Results. Soon after the Leadership 7.5 reorganization of Delta began, customer service ratings began to decline. On-time performance fell to one of the worst records in the industry. Mishandled baggage claims increased. Delta customers began to joke that the company name stood for "Doesn't ever leave the airport." As a Paine Webber analyst put it, "Morale fell a lot further than costs did." Union organizers began to find Delta a fertile ground for organizing. Employees who had made it through the cuts began to appear at work wearing Teamsters buttons. A company survey found that 48 percent of employees were unfavorably disposed to company leadership, with only 22 percent favorable. When Allen and other senior managers were rewarded for their successful restructuring efforts with massive bonuses, the hostile atmosphere intensified. Allen, who was fond of berating managers in front of their colleagues, won little support in the ranks of his immediate subordinates.

The other side of the coin. Delta Senior Vice President of Corporate Communications Thomas Slocum told the *Wall Street Journal* in an article about Allen's ouster that, "All these decisions that are no being called harsh and autocratic were made in the midst of hemorrhaging losses. If you're going to look at a man's management style, look at the results he led this company to."

Discussion points

1. Kathy Savitt of Seattle-based MWW/Savitt, says, "The problem with classic turnaround programs is that there is an overemphasis on cost management and an underemphasis on issues like corporate reputation and the relationship between a company and its key stakeholders. That means that a plan that looks good on paper can fail miserably once you try to implement it in the real world." Does her comment apply to the Delta case?

2. Another communications expert says of McKinsey, the consultant that helped Delta formulate the restructuring, "I could make a very nice living following McKinsey around and fixing all the human relations problems its approach creates." Is he giving McKinsey a "bad rap?"

3. It has been argued that communication is usually the last element considered as part of a restructuring program, when it should be the first. And the more of an afterthought communication is, the more time and money are needed to restore morale and rebuild culture—if they can be restored and rebuilt at all.

Update. Leo Mullin was selected by Delta's board to replace Ron Allen as the airline's chief executive officer. It was widely speculated that he would attempt to rebuild Delta's culture and expand the airline. In early 1998, the financial press was reporting that a merger of Delta with Continental Airlines was imminent. But at the last minute, on Super Bowl Sunday, Continental rejected the merger and instead announced that Northwest Airlines would buy a majority interest in Continental and merge the routes of the two carriers, while maintaining the identity and pilot seniority lists of both. Soon after, *Aviation Daily* reported that Mullin had told an American Bar Association group he was "upset at the misrepresentations" of Continental executives after they rejected the Delta deal. Mullin said he was initially told by Continental CEO Gordon Bethune that labor integration would not be a problem if Delta and Continental were merged. But later, Mullin said, Continental demanded a specific method of merging pilot seniority lists, which Mullin termed an "impossible condition" because of Delta's contract with its own pilots. Though Bethune has been quoted as blaming the "stupidity" of Delta management for the breakdown, Mullin alleged that it was Continental that had sought the deal, controlled the pace of talks and changed terms in nearly a month of discussions.

Discussion points:

1. Why would Delta's management care about pilot seniority if a profitable deal was on the table? Was it worth sinking the deal to keep a few pilots happy?

2. Discuss the Delta case in terms of each of the following eight steps in the public relations response process.

    a. Research.
    b. Set objectives.
    c. Identify key publics.
    d. Identify key media.

e Identify key messages.

f. Plan

g. Communicate and act.

h. Evaluate

REVIEW QUESTIONS AND EXERCISES

1. What kinds of information and data should the vice president communications of Delta have been monitoring to determine how the company's restructuring was affecting employee morale, AOBs and values?

2. You are the communications director for a company that wants to site a plant that will burn medical waste (including waste generated by AIDS patients). You want to site the incinerator in an area where there is a residential subdivision and a trailer park. The homes are of low value. Most of the residents are minority black Americans. You decide to announce the company's plans using only controlled mass media. What communications vehicles will you use to make the announcement? Is it likely that you'll be able to site the facility with a minimum of public opposition from the residents?

3. What are the key messages you will use in your campaign to reassure the public about the safety of the incinerator you hope to site in their neighborhood?

4. Are the commercial mass media that cover the neighborhood—the local newspapers, radio and television—likely to ignore your company's plans to site the incinerator? What's likely to get the commercial mass media interested in the story?

5. Would it be best to ignore the politicians elected to represent the incinerator neighborhood in your controlled media information effort? Isn't it best to "let sleeping dogs lie?"

CHAPTER FIVE

Start with the Employees

The landmark work of Larkin and Larkin summarizing contemporary research findings on change communication contends that three conditions must be present for effective communication with rank and file employees of large organizations: the communication needs to be face to face between first-line supervisor and subordinates, the communication needs to be one on one, and the communication needs to be about matters that affect the local workplace. Only this kind of communication will change behavior, they argue.

While Larkin and Larkin are primarily concerned with communicating change, their point applies as well to communicating with angry or outraged employees.

Arthur Page, America's first corporate p.r. vice president, of AT&T from 1927 to 1946, then America's largest corporation, early on in his tenure determined that employees were the single most important public with which the company needed to communicate. That was primarily because it was rank-and-file employees who had day-to-day contact with the customer public, and thereby created the attitudes, opinions and beliefs the public held toward the Bell System. Since about one of 100 gainfully employed Americans worked for the phone company during Page's tenure, and interacted with hundreds of constituents of the phone company each year, that made a lot of sense. But even if you work in an organization with far fewer employees than the Bell System enjoyed in its heyday, before the breakup and when

Bell was the nation's largest employer, it would be unwise ever to underestimate the importance of communication with employees.

THE CORPORATE WORLD IS LITTERED
WITH EMPLOYEE CASUALTIES

Corporate restructuring and downsizings, reengineering and profit maximization, and layoffs due to crisis have left employees as the most prominent casualties. They are frightened, suspicious and skeptical. They don't trust management—and perhaps for good reason. They feel, often erroneously, that managers don't care about anyone but themselves. They believe, perhaps incorrectly in many cases, that most managers would sell them out in a heartbeat for a few pieces of silver. Witness the adulation of Dilbert, the long-suffering employee perpetually abused by his pointy-haired boss.

Waves of change in the 1990s swept corporate America clean of deadwood, setting the stage for a runaway bull stock market. That was followed in 2000-2001 by a sharp recessionary correction. The reckless disregard in the 1990s for the welfare of employees who had grown accustomed to paternalistic cultures left them disgruntled, disenchanted, cynical and downright hostile. That mood was exacerbated by the wave after wave of layoffs that began in the 2000-2001 recessionary market correction.

Those who fail to deal with the emotions that are running rife in corporate America's employee ranks run the risk of further fueling a steady decline in employee morale, loss of productivity and substantial bottom-line losses. Employees are ready to mutiny, and it may well be the organization's leadership that walks the plank if the employees are not placated.

How bad is it? One recent survey of 700 employees at 70 companies found that:

• 54 percent said they "don't get decisions explained well."

• 61 percent said they "aren't well informed of organizational plans."

• And 64 percent said flatly they "don't believe what management tells them."

The frontline workforce is not populated by a mere handful of cynics. It is cynical through and through. According to a study by

Mervis and Kanter, as early as 1989 some 43 percent of employees believed that management cheats and lies, with the greatest amount of cynicism in the front ranks. It's gotten a lot worse since then. According to a 1994 Council of Communication Management survey reported in the *Wall Street Journal*, 64 percent of employees believed that management was lying. Two-thirds of the senior personnel managers surveyed by Right Associates in 1992 said that employees trust management less after a restructuring.

Employees in the past were largely loyal to the organizations for which they worked. That has changed. What they now feel is described by a *Wall Street Journal* reporter as follows: "They have been devastated by management's sudden attack on its most loyal supporters. Years of devotion and sacrifice now count for nothing. The fun is gone, replaced by chronic anxiety and fear."

Are workers really unhappy, or is that exaggeration? A recent study by Kempner-Tregoe found that fewer than half the workers questioned believed they or their fellow workers were happy. But when the managers of these employees were asked the same question, guess what? Two-thirds said they thought the workers were happy. Hey, guys and gals, what are you doing day after day in those ivory tower?

If you can't accept the importance of communicating with employees for any other reason, recognize that employee unrest affects the bottom line. One recent study of the cost of turmoil created in employee ranks by insensitive change poorly communicated sets the loss over three years at $3 million per 650 employees.

It is particularly important that leadership attend to communication. The Robert Half International recruiting firm says that CEOs should devote one-third of their time to building morale and productivity in the workforce.

THE FIVE KEYS TO A HAPPY WORKFORCE

Steve Rivkin of Rivkin & Associates, a marketing and communications consultancy that works with corporate clients, but especially hospitals populated by disgruntled, downsized workforces, says there are five keys to reviving employee trust and rekindling loyalty. They are:

• *Research.* You have to take the pulse of the workforce. Recognized that satisfied workers give better customer service. If workers are not happy, you need to know it. And don't kill the researcher for bringing you bad news.

• *Candor.* You must be honest and open in all your communication with the workforce. Employees like hearing the truth in person, face-to-face, in one on one meetings or small groups. They don't like to hear it in an e-mail or voice mail message, or slipped into a memo or newsletter.

• *Explain.* Answer the "why" when you announce a new policy. Why is AT&T going to lay off 18,000 people? Why is the purchasing function going to be outsourced? You have to treat employees as adults. Rivkin cites one worker in a focus group saying: "We run homes. We make decisions. We raise families. But when we go to work, it's like we don't know anything. Our boss won't let us make decisions. Our boss doesn't trust us."

• *Show some respect.* Rivkin says employees covet respect as much as money. In an Ernst and Young survey of senior managers and employees, 60 percent of the respondents thought they would be more motivated if they were treated as partners with managers rather than as hired hands. All too often, employees are made to feel like expendable commodities rather than as persons deserving of management's respect.

• *Leadership.* To lead, you need some idea of what employees expect of a leader. First, Rivkin argues, they want the quality of vision. That means setting an agenda and direction for the organization, and articulating it clearly to the rank and file. The best leaders, Rivkin says, are storytellers, cheerleaders, facilitators. They reinforce the vision with communication and action. The other important ingredient in the leader is character. What is character? It's not the opinion others have of you. Rather, it's what you really are. Perhaps the trait of character employees most want in the leader is caring. How do you demonstrate the character employees admire? By demonstrating your commitment to your industry, your concern for your organization and your sincere caring for employees.

The bottom line in creating a happy workforce, according to Rivkin, is that the leader must deeply care about those he or she leads. Those who advocate the re-engineering of organizations might of course disagree, contending the mark of a leader is to eliminate deadwood and maximize profit.

AVOID COMMUNICATING VALUES

We know that all humans, including our employees, have attitudes, opinions, beliefs and values. While organizations are not
people, the people in the organizations frequently adopt values
for the organization. These become placards, wallet cards, posters and any number of other communication devices designed
to be hung, posted or filed where they can be totally ignored—or,
occasionally, become the focus of jokes or outrage.

One of the most common mistakes managers make in communicating is to attempt to wrap change in values. These values are most often written in ambitious statements of vision,
mission and principles. Consultant Jim Lukaszewski calls these
pronouncements, which litter the walls of gray flannel America,
the "corporate vegetables." Employees value them about as much
as they value a plate full of cauliflower, broccoli and brussels
sprouts.

Why do these grandiose statements fail? Simply put, because
of a truth you learned in the sandbox: that actions speak louder
than words. If a used-car salesman handed you a business card
that says, "We value our customers," would you believe that?
Probably not. You'd probably think, "This guy would probably try
to sell me a bag of garbage on four wheels, guaranteeing it to be
the fifth wonder of the world that will do everything I want, so
long as he doesn't have to put it in writing." What you would
respect is demonstrated action on the salesman's part to provide you with a great car at a reasonable price, plus excellent
service, all the while performing in your interest above and beyond the call of commission.

Today's organizational managers often have less credibility
than used-car salesmen. Those who do have the admiration and
respect of the rank and file have usually learned to avoid the
value talk. That can be a difficult decision, given a Wyatt study
that found 68 percent of large companies consider missions and
values to be their number one communication priority.

All too often, reductions in force and other actions that poi-
sonously threaten the security of rank and file employees are
accompanied by the issuance of new company mission statements, or cloaked in the verbiage of existing visions and delu-
sions. Little wonder that such statements are little respected by
employees. Further, the omnipresent statements of corporate

aspirations remain constantly visible to employees who compare their ambitious goals to corporate reality. All too often, reality falls far short of the organizational aspiration hammered out between rounds of golf and paintball at a weeklong leadership team retreat at a posh resort.

As Larkin and Larkin put it, "The only effective way to communicate a value is to act in accordance with it and give others the incentive to do the same." If a company values communicating honestly with employees, then pay and promotion should be awarded to those who communicate effectively, rather than to those who equivocate, weave and dodge, pander and prevaricate. If you value customer service, then recruitment, performance appraisals, promotions and bonuses should go to those who walk the walk, not to those who talk the talk.

Cloaking a new organizational policy or procedure in a value or mission statement is sure to evoke employee suspicion. Employees are not dumb. Like managers, they learned in the sandbox that actions are what's important, not words. Talking about values signals to them that fraud and lies are near.

Is it possible that employees could be wrong, and that value and mission statements actually do play an important role in accomplishing corporate goals? Hardly. Already in 1992, the Jensen group, which specializes in communication designed to facilitate change, studied 23 large U.S. companies including American Express, AT&T, Chemical Bank, IBM, Johnson & Johnson, Mobil and Texaco. Seventy percent of the corporations had revised their corporate missions during recent restructurings (read downsizings). Only nine percent of the companies felt that revising their mission helped them to achieve the objectives of the restructuring.

The lesson is clear. Your message is more likely to be received positively if you avoid cloaking bad news in mission statements and management proclamations.

FAILING TO COMMUNICATE
ENCOURAGES RUMORS

Failure to communicate with employees during major organizational changes, when emotions are likely to be running high, is one of the worst mistakes an organization can make. Studies of the role of communication during mergers and acquisitions, another time of employee concern, show clearly that in times of stress and uncertainty, people fill communication voids with rumors. Rumors end up assigning the worst possible motives to those in charge—those who stand to benefit the most.

Why do employees bother with rumors in times of stress? Communication helps to lower anxiety—not just for females, by the way, although studied indicate that women use communication more than males to relieve anxiety. Even if the news is bad, employees will communicate it. Yes, we humans do seek to find pleasure and to avoid pain. When it comes to communication in times of stress, uncertainty is even more painful than bad news, so the bad news moves like wildfire on the grapevine.

Regarding rumors, remember that they more often contain negative than positive information. Research indicates that a negative statement is on average ten times more powerful than a positive statement, ten times more likely to be believed and remembered. It takes a lot of positive communication to overcome the damage done by even a minor negative rumor.

FACE-TO-FACE COMMUNICATION IS BEST

It's change that most often upsets employees, so it's usually change that has to be dealt with in communication with angry or outraged employees. Research indicates clearly that the best way to communicate change is face-to-face from the supervisor to the employee. Employees want to get the word from their bosses, not from other employees. They want to get it from a person, not from reading an e-mail, not from listening to a voice mail, not from seeing it on the company Intranet or Internet. They don't want to read it in a company newspaper, and they don't want to hear it from a company video.

Remember that the lower the echelon of the company with which you are seeking to communicate, the greater the cynicism is likely to be. You have to reach front-line employees through their supervisors. And the supervisors will tell you they don't want to talk to employees in a group if the topic is unpopular. That just sets them up to be embarrassed by the biggest critic in the group—especially if the supervisor is not on the company hot-line with all the answers to what is really going on.

What does all this suggest? When emotions are high, communicate face-to-face, supervisor to employee, one-on-one.

That does not mean that company publications and videos are worthless. Videos can be valuable in communicating technical information. Publications play an important role in providing recognition and in guiding face-to-face communication. But when you want to change the behavior of employees, when you want to reduce emotions, it's face-to-face one-on-one supervisor-subordinate communication that works best.

Large meetings have their place in the communication arsenal as well. They're especially good for providing recognition to employees who have reached safety and service benchmarks, been promoted or done something else worthy of note. When it comes to communicating controversial information, however, supervisors know to avoid them like the plague. In "Why Supervisors Resist Employee Involvement," a 1984 inquiry into how supervisors like to communicate, Janice A. Klein reported that 85 percent of supervisors avoided group meetings, preferring one-on-one communication. She found that the supervisors knew from experience that group meetings quickly degenerate into grievance sessions.

One on one, employees can be reasonable and cooperative. In a group, the dynamics change. In the group, any employee who stands up to support a management initiative is going to be branded a brown-noser or worse. And what supervisor is dumb enough to ask a group of rank-and-file workers to support an unpopular management initiative? The supervisor didn't get to where he or she is by being dumb. He or she will profess support for an unpopular idea to superiors, but will react differently once those superiors are out of range and it's the factory-floor employees that the supervisor has to face.

If you really want to communicate in a way that encourages employees to change behavior—to support reorganization or a new program—then provide information to first-line supervisors and let them pass it on to subordinates in one-on-one meetings.

Employees have been making it clear in communication research for years that they would rather receive information from their immediate supervisors than from senior managers. Larkin and Larkin recommend that organizations spend 80 percent of their communication dollars on getting supervisors prepared to communicate with the employees who report to them.

MAKING COMMUNICATORS OUT
OF FIRST-LINE SUPERVISORS

It's commonly believed that to be effective communicators, people have to be trained. That's nonsense. We all learned how to communicate in the sandbox. Supervisors already know how to communicate. They communicate daily with their subordinates. They may not always communicate in the most tactful terms possible, but they do communicate.

What supervisors do need is information. One way to provide the information they need, and to gain their support as well, is to hold supervisor briefings.

It's important that two-way communication be involved in the supervisor meetings. Suppose an organization is considering the introduction of change—a change in the organization itself, or a program designed to change the behavior of employees. Let a senior manager from the change team brief a small group of supervisors whose work groups will be affected by the change. In this phase, supervisors are told about the change and permitted to make recommendations. The senior manager reports the recommendations to the change team, and that group tries to work as many of the recommendations as possible into the change plan. The more recommendations that get worked into the final plan, the more likely the supervisors will be to support the change.

In the second phase, the senior manager reports to the supervisors on the adoption of the recommendations and explains the final plan. After this, the change is rolled out, usually accompanied by stories in the company newsletter, fact sheets and perhaps a videotape.

MINI-CASE: NAVISTAR CHANGES ITS CULTURE

Situation. Navistar International was the name selected in the 1980s for what was left of International Harvester after it sold off its farm equipment business and the IH name with it. What was left was a truck and engine company. In what could be thought of as a restructuring, Navistar's workforce was reduced from 110,000 people in the mid-1980s to 15,000 in 1997. The company's stock price dropped in the same period from the mid-forties to less than $10. What was left of the employee workforce was heavily unionized and had an antagonistic, adversarial relationship with management. It was from this low that the company set out on the path to renewal.

The CEO. John Horne became Navistar's president and CEO in 1992, and its president, chairman and CEO in 1996. A veteran who joined the old International Harvester in 1966 as an engineer, he rose through the ranks. Throughout his career, he had a deep passion for the company.

The diagnosis. At the time Horne became CEO of Navistar, the company was one of the worst-performing in the United States. Maril McDonald, who joined Navistar in 1993 and became vice president of corporate communications in 1995, diagnosed what was wrong with Navistar as "a collective lack of self-esteem." The company was so battered, she thinks, that it lacked the sense of crisis that is necessary to spur change. Employees from the rank and file factory floor workers to executives had come to see mere survival as a goal. They were more interested in surviving than in changing and prospering.

The twin sisters of culture change. The literature of cultural change suggests that two conditions are necessary for successful change. One is that the organization recognizes that a state of crisis exists—employees, managers and leadership are convinced that what has worked in the past will not work in the future. The second is that change needs to be driven from the top, by a CEO who can make managers accept the necessity of change. Neither of these conditions existed at Navistar, drawing into question the validity of research.

The change process begins. The process of changing Navistar began when members of the communications team went to employees and in focus groups asked them how they could be more productive. Says communications chief MacDonald, "The information we got was revealing... Employees said that they could help achieve the company's goals better if they knew what the goals were. But... (m)ost of their concerns and recommendations revolved around the culture of the company, how Navistar was run and managed." Employees pretty well knew what needed to be done to make the company work, but had "heard it all before" from executives who had came out and talked to the factory floor about change. Employees were skeptical, asking why they should believe that this time would be different. MacDonald's answer was that they could not be certain, but why not try to change the culture anyway?

The role of the CEO. MacDonald took the findings of the focus groups to CEO Horne. He was emphatic about not wanting a new culture driven from the top down. Rather, he wanted a culture driven from the bottom up. He asked only that new culture emphasize high performance and respect for the individual.

Research continues. The Communications Team's original findings from the focus groups were reinforced and validated by one-on-one interviews and written surveys of the workforce. The findings: employees thought the company was lacking in three key core areas: direction, teamwork and trust.

Getting managers to buy in. As a next step, the Communications Team developed a template in which four different corporate cultures were displayed. Company A was a strict authoritarian company where all decisions were made at the top, employees had no discretion, and employees were told only what management thought they ought to know. Company B was one where employees were given ownership and responsibilities, encouraged to participate in decisions and information was communicated and shared freely. Companies C and D on the template were variants of company B, but with an even more collegial, consensus-oriented cultures. Managers were quick to recognize the culture of Company A as Navistar's culture. They quickly bought in to the idea of changing the Navistar culture to a variant of Company B with some elements of Companies C and D. The 30 or so top managers were then required to prepare reports on what needed to be done in their areas to change Navistar to a Type B culture. These reports were presented to the CEO and the other managers.

The next steps. After the new culture was presented to the CEO, Navistar called a meeting of 450 mid-level managers. At the meeting, actors played out scenes from the company's everyday operations highlighting what was wrong with the old culture—obstructive bureaucracy, pointless rules, lack of communication. Then, the 30 senior managers took the stage and performed a rap. Next came a serious discussion of what was wrong with the corporate culture and what needed to change. Now the subject of culture change was on the table for discussion. Following that, a three-day management meeting was held in which cross-functional teams discussed Navistar's mission and values. Seven major values emerged: respect for people; customer focus; relentless pursuit of quality; speed, simplicity, agility; innovation; accountability; and communication. Behaviors appropriate to each value were also identified.

Relations with the union. Navistar's employee relations to a large extent revolved around relations with the United Auto Workers. When the communications team prepared its first Speak Up employee opinion survey, it met with the UAW bargaining committee before distributing it. The union leadership had two concerns: first, that it might raise employee expectations only to let them down once again, and second, that management in the past had conducted surveys but not shared the results with employees. A union member was invited to join the Communications Team and approve the wording of the survey. The member had no objections to any of the questions, including those that sampled employee opinions about the union. The survey was distributed, and results came back. They were not favorable to management.

Communications changes. As the cultural changes rolled out, communication at Navistar adapted. Speed in disseminating information became important. Substance took precedence over form. Direct communication took precedence over indirect. Financial information flowed more freely to rank and file employees, along with information about how employee performance can affect bottom-line financial performance. Workshops were held to provide training and improve communication. The 450 members of the company's leadership council went through a Climate for Performance workshop.

Results: Navistar went from being an ailing to a turnaround company. The company's stock hovered in the $9 to $10 range through 1996. Then, as the results of the restructuring impacted on the company's bottom line and earnings began to climb dramatically, the stock's price exploded. By early 1998, it was trading in the low $30s, a 300 percent gain. Net income per share in the quarter ended in January 1998 (the company's fiscal year ends in October), was 42 cents per share, up 320 percent from a year earlier. The First Call forecast for Navistar's fiscal year ending in October 1998 was for $2.31 per share, up 40 percent, with further growth forecast for fiscal 1999. Then, however, the company began to fade as the momentum for change petered out. Today, Navistar is not much better off than it was when its reinvention was still just a glimmer in the imaginations of a few executives.

Discussion points:

1. Is there evidence that first-line supervisors bought into the change at Navistar? Did first-line supervisors play an important role in changing Navistar's culture?

2. Was there an explosion of anger among rank-and-file employees or the union over the changes? If not, why not?

3. Lazarsfeld, Berelson and Gaudet conducted pioneering research in the 1940s into the role of opinion leaders in communication. Who are the likely opinion leaders at Navistar?

4. If Navistar is back to ground zero, the point at which it was before re-engineering, was their any point to the re-invention of the corporation? Was it all just useless flailing to make managers look busy?

REVIEW QUESTIONS AND EXERCISES

1. Where do employees get the idea that their managers would sell them out in a heartbeat? Is there any truth in the satire of the Dilbert comic strip? Do you have any firsthand evidence from your own experience?

2. How do you measure the cost of employee outrage and anger on the bottom line of the business?

3. Your company has decided to reduce employee ranks by 2,000. Management has decided the best way to do that is to issue a new mission statement emphasizing the company's need to react quickly to new market pressures by adjusting its workforce accordingly. As director of communications, what is your advice to management?

4. Do you believe the research finding that a negative statement is 10 times more likely to be believed and remembered than a positive statement? Does this have any bearing on the need to control rumors when employees are angry or outraged about something that is happening in the workplace?

5. Management plans to introduce a major downsizing by showing a video. First-line supervisors will be asked to show the video to employee meetings. At the end of the video, employees

who have questions are to call them to a company hot line phone bank set up by the Communication Team. Is this the best way to introduce the change?

REFERENCES, RESOURCES AND SUGGESTIONS FOR FURTHER READING

Larkin, T.J., and Sandar Larkin. *Communicating Change: Winning Employee Support for New Business Goals.* New York: McGraw-Hill, 1994.

Larkin, T.J., and Sandar Larkin. "Reaching and Changing Front-line Employees." *Harvard Business Review,* May-June 1996, pp. 95-104.

Rivkin, Steve. "Mutiny in the Cafeteria." *The Public Relations Strategist* 3:4 (Winter 1998), pp. 20-23.

CHAPTER SIX

Working with the Media
in Risk Situations

The mass media can be of great assistance in a crisis situation. They can also be a hindrance. This chapter discusses the nature of the media and makes suggestions for working effectively with reporters covering a risk situation.

THE IMPORTANCE OF RAPID RESPONSE
AND DAMAGE CONTROL

One of the measures of a presidential administration in the United States is its performance in the first 100 days.

The new administration of President George W. Bush in 2001 gave the nation an object lesson in how much rapid response and damage control have to do with reducing outrage and creating favorable impressions. The performance was in sharp contrast to the harried first days of the Clinton administration, characterized by bungled responses to a series of public relations problems such as the alleged political favoritism involved in restructuring of the White House Travel Office.

In power for just three weeks, President Bush and his rapid response team fixed their mistakes almost as quickly as they made them.

The first crisis surfaced just before Inauguration Day with revelations that a Cabinet nominee had employed an illegal alien. The nominee, Linda Chavez, was quickly cast adrift by an angry

George W. Bush whose team had not been informed of the alien. The new President made it known that he would not defend the nominee, who ended up staging her own news conference in which she withdrew her nomination. Only three days elapsed from the first revelations to the withdrawal.

Next, an announcement that the White House offices of civil rights and AIDS would be closed was quickly retracted and the offices restored before gay and civil rights groups could mount protests. Within hours of the report appearing in *USA Today*, the tempest was bottled up by Press Secretary Ari Fleischer, who said the President's chief of staff had been wrong.

Democratic consultant Jim Duffy explained, "The Bushies respond so quickly and don't worry about how to spin it out. They say, 'We screwed up. We're going to fix it.' They're more into getting about their work than worrying about how the news will play out that day."[1]

Similarly, the Bush public relations team worked behind the scenes to smooth out problems with a bipartisan patients' rights bill, the proposed $1.6 trillion tax-cut package and the nomination of conservative John Ashcroft's confirmation as attorney general.

All this augered that when a real crisis erupted, the Bush Administration would be prepared. That major crisis came on the morning of September 11, 2001, when four airliners were hijacked by terrorists. Two of the planes were piloted directly into the twin towers of the World Trade Center, while a third crashed into the Pentagon in a third suicidal kamikaze attack. Thousands of American lives were lost in the terrorist actions.

President Bush and high level officials responded to the crisis in a manner that won overwhelming support from the American people. On the Saturday before the terrorist attacks, the President's approval rating had been 56%. From the first day, the President reacted calmly and compassionately but decisively to the crisis, effectively communicating through the mass media what the Administration was thinking and doing. By the Friday following the attack, his rating was up 30 points to 86 percent. That is not to say that he plays to the opinion polls. It's notable that he does not. According to those who know him, including his pollsters, he abhors making decisions based on surveys. He ignores them, and rather depends on the advice of expert advisors for input when making decisions. The point here is that being prepared to react wisely to crisis, and then communicating those actions effectively through the mass media, rather than remaining inactive and noncommunicative, plays a very important role in garnering public approval.

The reaction of the American public to the terrorist attacks was justifiable outrage. President George W. Bush's Administration proved adept at channeling that public anger to constructive ends, uniting the nation in support of impending retaliation. Channeling anger and outrage to constructive ends is what this book is all about. This chapter discusses techniques for working with the media in outrage situations.

CHARACTERISTICS OF MASS MEDIA CRISIS COVERAGE

When faced with reporting about confrontations with angry individuals or outraged publics, organizations are likely to believe they are being treated unfairly or downright meanly. That's because, except for the public relations people on staff, most employees or organizations aren't familiar with the way mass media, and especially reporters, go about covering the news.

Following are some points about reporting worth keeping in mind when your organization is in the news during a confrontation or crisis.

Are reporters biased or just writing with a viewpoint?

Recognize that much of the news, perhaps as much as half of it, doesn't originate with reporters paid by the media but with public relations people who feed information to the media.

Of what is left, some stories originate with news services such as the Associates Press, and only a small portion come from the on-staff reporters or newscasters of the local media. Of this portion, yes, a small part of the reporting is from a viewpoint or shows reportorial bias.

Reporting with bias or viewpoint is not new to America. Loading media coverage with a point of view is as old as our national media establishment. Some benchmarks:

• The Colonial press in America was a press with a strong viewpoint. Advocacy, not objectivity, was the order of the day.

Depending on the political leanings of a publisher, the newspaper was likely to revile the monarchy or defend the king at the expense of local patriots. This bent toward covering news from a viewpoint continued through the Civil War.

• With the advent of the penny press and mass circulation newspapers in the 1890s, objectivity came to characterize many news items, with viewpoints reserved for editorials and columns. That's not to deny that decisions about what news to cover were still made by editors with an eye to readership.

• Early in the 20th century, with newspapers increasingly paying pious attention to objectivity, muckraking with a viewpoint became popular in magazines such as *McClure's*.

• Later in the century, radio and then television news tended to embrace the objectivity ethic, with the exception of documentaries such as Edward R. Murrow's "Harvest of Shame" and its imitator magazine-format programs like "60 Minutes," which reported with a viewpoint.

• Then, in the late 1960s, a young crop of magazine and newspaper journalists led by writers such as Gail Sheehy and Tom Wolfe re-embraced advocacy journalism.

The point: mass media in America have a long tradition of reporting with a viewpoint.

In a crisis, journalists want to be where the story is.

In times of crisis, journalists gravitate to where to story is happening. That may be the scene of a disaster hundreds of miles away, a church sanctuary on the south side of town, or simply the floor where the main newsroom is located. The reporters and editors congregate and begin producing the written and graphic images the public expects from a news outlet.

When a major crisis such as the attack on New York and Washington of September 2001 is breaking, reporters who normally specialize become beat reporters. A sports reporter may go to the crisis site to interview rescue workers and survivors. A fashion reporter might interview a local minister on why God permits tragedy and the prayers the cleric thinks appropriate.

In such a situation, the news staffers at media outlets drop whatever they're doing and become part of a seamless team process of producing tomorrow's history.

During crises, the public's attention to the media escalates. On the day of the 2001 terrorist air attacks on the World Trade Center and Pentagon, the afternoon edition of the normally moribund Atlanta *Journal* sold nearly 65,000 additional copies. The next morning's edition of the Atlanta *Constitution* sold an additional 127,000 copies—and this in a society that gets most of its news from television!

They call 'em "newspapers," not "truthpapers"

Don't expect the media to be overly kind to you during a disaster or crisis if you're at fault. Journalists will generally report favorably so long as you are performing in the public interest. But when a crisis occurs, especially if your organization appears to be performing contrary to what reporters perceive as the public interest, the reporters are more likely to communicate viewpoint in their coverage.

Crisis are events out of the ordinary routine. That's what makes them news. News gets covered. And never forget—they do call them *news*papers, not *truth*papers.

Reporters use "objective" to mean "balanced"

Even when journalists talk of being objective, they are not talking about objectivity in the same way a scientist might use the term. A reporter doesn't use the term "objectivity" to mean "absolute, empirical, replicable truth." The journalist uses objectivity as a synonym for "balance." For the journalist, a story is balanced if it criticizes an institution, but quotes the institution in a few paragraphs that give the institution's side of the story or issue. A reporter is even more likely to say a story is objective if it gives equal weight to each conflicting claim, allowing the reader to draw his or her own conclusions.

What does that mean to you? It means that a reporter will probably be willing to give your side of an issue coverage, so long as you are credible and have a moderate rather than extreme position on an issue. Following are some guidelines to follow when providing reporters with information to balance their stories:

• Don't wait for a reporter to call you if an issue in which you have an interest has become topical. Call to let the reporter know your viewpoint.

• When discussing your organization's view of the issue, don't take an extreme position. Reporters are far more likely to discuss moderate positions pro or con on an issue than views at either extreme. And don't take a politician's middle of the road stance—"we're for it and we're against it"—either. Reporters aren't likely to cover viewpoints in the wishy-washy middle of an issue.

• If your organization is in the middle of a crisis such as a large petroleum spill or chemical emission into the air, reporters will find their way to you for information and quotes. You can contact them if you wish. The easiest way is by putting out a media advisory through the nearest office of the Associated Press. But rest assured that the media will find you with or without your help unless you go into hiding.

Why reporters sometimes get it wrong

Many consumers of mass media news have a tendency to believe pretty much everything offered to them, although a healthy strain of skepticism is developing. Scholars who study the mass media know the truth, that news reports are usually lightly sprinkled with error.

Back in the 11 years the author taught journalism at the Universities of Wisconsin and Georgia, he did some research on the accuracy of newspaper stories. He found that the typical six-inch story contained 1.6 accuracy errors. About half the errors were objective (facts such as someone's name or age was wrong) and half were subjective (the newsmaker felt the reporter told only part of the story or slanted the facts).

To a large extent, the errors in media coverage are due to deadline pressures. To a lesser extent, they are the result of a system that rewards reporters not for being right but for being prompt, for meeting deadlines and being the first to report news. But it's not that simple.

General assignment reporters are often called upon to cover subjects about which they know little or nothing. The typical general assignment reporter is more often than not a journalism school graduate. Except for television news anchors in major markets, the reporters are not paid particularly highly. Reporters at small dailies may make as little as $15,000 to $25,000 per year.

This typical general assignment reporter while in college will have had no more science courses than he or she was required to take to graduate. A typical reporter might have had two science courses, chosen carefully (astronomy 101, or "Stars," for example) to avoid anything particularly difficult.

The professors who teach these fledgling journalists often have only a master's or even bachelor's degree, with a little media reporting experience to countervail the degree(s) they're short. Four of these doctorless teachers on a committee are no match for a single history professor with a Ph.D. The journalism professors who do have Ph.D.'s are often devoid of practical reporting experience, having gone straight through bachelor's, master's and Ph.D. degrees without venturing into the real reportorial world. The Ph.D.'s are often the product of diploma mills that stress pointless research that mostly makes a professor proficient in a publish or perish but not pragmatic world.

The hapless underpaid general assignment reporter may be a frustrated creative writer who wants to write the great American novel or the great American movie script. He or she needs to make a living while doing (or thinking about doing) creative writing on the side.

The small daily reporter is typically assigned two to three stories a day. While the reporter is writing a story about your organization, he or she may be thinking about the story that has to be written next. His or her goal may well be to learn just enough to write a credible piece about your organization rather than to learn everything possible about your story.

Finally, there are negative penalties for reporters who let competitors get the news out ahead of them. No reporter wants to be "scooped," incurring the wrath of his or her boss.

All these factors contribute to the inaccuracy of news coverage. But despite all the pressures toward inaccuracy, what comes out of the American news media is remarkably accurate.

As a rule rather than an exception, knowledgeable reporters are assigned to beats or "special assignment reporting" such as the environment or business areas. If a specialized reporter is not assigned to your story, it will usually be worth your while to work with the beat journalists whom you can expect to write regularly about your organization.

The story will be covered whether or not you provide input

One of the mistakes CEOs and novice public information officers often make is to assume that if they avoid the media, there will be no story. Rest assured, if a crisis occurs, there will be a story on the local and perhaps the national news whether your organization contributes to the story or not.

Reporters are paid to fill a hole—a three-minute hole in the evening tv news, a 12-inch hole in the newspaper, a 35-second spot in the radio news. They're going to fill that hole to earn their paycheck whether or not your organization cooperates.

Reporters work for bylines as well as salary

Journalists work for rewards other than pay just like the rest of us. They work, for example, for the bylines or air time that gives them recognition. And they work for the awards that permit them to get ahead in their careers. Reporting with a viewpoint in longer stories and series is usually what wins them the awards, so when continuing stories or front page news is breaking, you need to be doing the most to cooperate with and meet the needs of these reporters.

When big stories are breaking, reporters are especially interested in talking to you. It's at these times that reporters most often write "color stories." In a color story, the journalist reports on the fears of victims or neighbors, the views of ideologues, the speculations of spokespeople and the history of an organization's mismanagement.

NOT ALL RISK STORIES ARE BIG NEWS

Every day, a few stories are selected to make the front page of the newspaper and the opening teasers for the evening television news. How do the gatekeepers at the media make the decisions about which stories get covered?

Wire services such as the Associated Press provide subscribers with summaries rank-ordering the stories that are the most important that day. The daily AP agenda of important stories is likely to have considerable influence with media gatekeepers—especially insofar as selection of national and international news for local editions is concerned.

Gatekeepers frequently monitor agenda-setting media such as the Cable News Network (CNN) and *New York Times* to see what stories they are covering. Radio station newscasters may "rip and read" from the local morning newspaper, and in the process influence television news assignment editors who are making their decisions about what is important. The television assignment editors dispatching television news crews in the morning have their own good ideas of what meetings and other events will be worth sending news crews to cover for that day's evening news. Editorial boards meet and make decisions about the stories that will make the front pages of the next edition of each newspaper section. Finally, some events are so big—a tornado touching down in town, a juicy murder trial—that even the village idiot would know that the media audience is hungry for information about the subject.

The media tend to over-cover some topics and undercover others. They tend to over-cover whatever "sells newspapers" or "brings in the audience during ratings sweeps." They over-cover crime (which poses a risk to the potential victim public) because crime both interests and frightens their audiences. That guarantees readership, listenership and viewership. The commercial media are in the business of delivering audience to advertisers. Reporting on crime may be sensationalistic, but it builds audience. Ever wonder why stories like "Our town's illicit sex industry" crop up on the local television news during ratings weeks? Stories like that attract viewers. Viewers are what the television station sells to advertisers. All the media—even the Public Broadcasting System and National Public Radio—are in business to perpetuate themselves by making money. The commercial media are more aggressive in their quest to make more bucks than NPR, and NPR is a little less aggressive, that's all

The media tend to understate many other risks, especially if the gatekeepers don't have a clue regarding how large a slice of the public is actually at risk. Yes, petroleum spills, train derailments and truck accidents involving hazardous materials will get extensive coverage. Those subjects represent familiar ground. A subject like radon, however, is less familiar and less likely to get covered—unless, of course, public outrage is involved, in which case the media are back on familiar ground.

Never lie, never guess

While they may not be penalized for it, reporters don't like being wrong. It subjects them to criticism from the public, and more likely, from higher-ups at the news medium where they work. But mostly, reporters don't like being wrong for the same reasons you and I like to be right.

If you lie to a reporter, or if you guess at the facts and get them wrong, and the reporter reports the incorrect information only to hear about it from a subscriber or a boss, you create problems for yourself. If you lie, the reporter may never believe you again. If you get the facts wrong, your credibility with the reporter will suffer. Credibility, believability and trust are powerful correlates. Lose one and you lose the others.

There's a simple solution. Never lie. Stick to the truth. And never guess at the facts or speculate about the facts. If you don't know the answer, say you don't. Then go try to find the answer and pass it along to the reporter who asked the question.

What if you know the correct facts but are not at liberty to reveal them? Tell the reporter you're not free to communicate the answer. If you are able, tell the reporter why you can't answer the question. The reporter might not like being denied the information, but will respect you.

Never ask for kills

Public relations professional should never ask the journalists for a story to be killed. Neither should a local politician or businessperson, for that matter, but journalists are likely to regard the sin as more egregious if committed by a public relaitons professinal. Asking a reporter at a major daily or television station to kill a story will likely provoke a hostile response. Threatening the reporter with dire consequences, such as the withdrawal of advertising, will more likely provoke the reporter to a more adversarial stance than would have been the case if you'd let the reporter alone.

If your credibility is low, start with the trades

The trade press is less adversarial than the commercial press. Reporters there come closer to being friends of the industries they cover than in any other case.

If your organization's credibility and trust ratings with the mass media are low because of something that has happened, a good place to begin rebuilding that credibility and trust is with the trade press. That's what the public relations director of Jack in the Box restaurants did after undercooked hamburgers containing *e. coli* bacteria were responsible for several fatalities at the firm's outlets. It took about two years of building from the trades before the commercial mass media became interested in covering Jack in the Box in a favorable light again.

THE MASS MEDIA
AND REPORTING OF RISK INFORMATION

Following are some generalizations about the reporting of risk information by the mass media.

To get a risk story out fast, go to radio first

If you have a crisis that requires a public evacuation, demands that people stay indoors, not drink the water or avoid open flame or sparks, radio can probably get the story out faster than other media. Television is the second-fastest medium for disseminating emergency information, followed by daily newspapers, weekly newspapers and magazines.

Controlled media such as letters and newsletters can be distributed quickly in targeted neighborhoods if you have the manpower and transportation.

Remember that you may need local law enforcement officials, the fire department, the HAZMAT team or even the National Guard to help you make rapid public notifications.

Reporters are not particularly interested in risk information

If you're involved in the unauthorized release of a hazardous substance–in a petroleum spill or a chemical release into the air, for example–reporters will likely be more interested in basic facts than they will be in reporting information about risk. The basic facts are such things as who did it, what happened, when it happened, where it happened, why it happened, and what's being done about it. It won't always occur to the reporter to cover information such as how toxic the substance is, the degree of danger posed and related information—unless, of course, people are dropping over dead in the streets. Take gasoline, for example. In addition to properties of flammability, it can asphyxiate, it can kill flora and fauna and some of its ingredients are carcinogens. Would you think to ask about these latter properties at a gasoline spill site if you were a novice reporter?

If you have information about the toxicity of a material that was accidentally released and the precautions people should take, such as avoiding well water until tests have been conducted, volunteer this information to the reporter. If you don't, the reporter may not ask, and the information may go unreported—at least until well into the event, when the reporter gets interested in a follow-up story and needs new information, but too late for the information to be of value to those affected.

Reporters are more interested in crisis than in chronic risk

While a fire is still burning, a reporter may be interested in the risk created by chemicals in the smoke. If the smoke contains carcinogens such as polycyclic aromatic hydrocarbons, for example, the reporter may give a few paragraphs to this information.

Smoke from barbecue grills also contains polycyclic aromatic hydrocarbons. Exposure to the smoke at backyard barbecues over the years poses a chronic risk. A reporter is not likely to be much interested in that unless he or she is doing a background piece on cancer—or on the dangers of backyard cooking.

If your organization is the American Cancer Society, and you're trying to alert the public to the dangers of polycyclic aromatic hydrocarbons created when fat from meat drops on coals and creates smoke, you'll probably have to work to market the information to the media. Look for a news peg with which to lead your story—the reporter needs something newsworthy on which to hang the rest of the material. Perhaps a pseudo-event where a local newsmaker barbecues a whole pig might make a peg.

Whatever the peg, make it interesting and newsworthy. Perhaps you can make the story more marketable by introducing controversy into it. However you choose to market such information, don't expect the reporter to turn cartwheels. He or she will probably remain predisposed more to covering crisis than chronic risk.

Reporters have to simplify issues

Newsmakers tend to be more critical of subjective than objective error in news coverage.

One of the major factors contributing to subjective error is the journalist's need to simplify issues. Reporters know that they have to simplify complex information into simple facts that readers or viewers can quickly grasp. This tendency to oversimplify often offends people who are well informed on a specific issue.

Part of the reason reporters do not seek out experts on a subject, and instead rely for quotes on the people who are directly involved in a controversy, is that they are used to experts who hedge statements, refuse to take sides or make clear-cut judgments. Reporters see this as unwillingness to commit. When a news source hedges between a clear-cut "yes" or "no," the reporter will often continue to ask questions until the newsmaker can be quoted on one side or the other of an issue.

Reporters tend to be especially reluctant to extensively quote authorities who expound in depth on the complexities of issues.

Newsmakers often resent the pressure from journalists to make them take stances on issues. The newsmakers know that issues usually aren't simple, and that there are no clear-cut answers or solutions.

While all that may be true, the reporter has to simplify the issues, if not for the least common denominator in the audience, then at least for the median or average reader. If a newsmaker doesn't simplify the issue, the reporter probably will, at the risk of introducing subjective error into the story.

Reporters like to function as early warning systems

Reporters as a class believe they have a responsibility to alert the public to danger. They see themselves as early warning systems.

In cases of emergencies such as chemical spills, the reporter's duty to inform the public of dangers is clear-cut. Even in such situations, however, the reporter may choose or edit content so as to reduce public alarm and the potential for panic. Such was the case in coverage of the Three Mile Island disaster, in which a meltdown almost occurred. A Presidential commission found in a content analysis of the first-week news coverage of the accident that some 73 percent was reassuring, and only 27 percent alarming in tone and content.

It's in the area of chronic risk that reporters are more unlikely to warn the public of dangers. When a building is burning or an overturned rail car is leaking an explosive material, the risk is clear. In the case of a pesticide used on apples that might cause cancer, the risk is not nearly so clear.

Reporters tend to see in black and white, not shades of gray

Reporters tend to dichotomize coverage of controversies, to divide stories into two sides and then try to balance the coverage of each side. That means they see things as either black or white, not in shades of gray. When it comes to risk involved in an accident, or the risk involved in a facility being placed in a neighborhood where some or all residents oppose the facility, reporters will likely quote one set of individuals who say the situation is safe, and another set saying the situation is unsafe or hazardous. This tendency to convert stories about complex issues into simple bipolar controversies is particularly apparent in television news coverage. When a reporter has only 40 seconds to tell a story, he or she doesn't have time to portray all the shades of gray between the dichotomous positions.

Is it there or not?

One of the big problems in dealing with reporters about the presence of toxic substances in the water, air or earth is the "is it there?" dilemma. Let's say you've had a petroleum release into groundwater from a leaking underground storage tank. You're finding hydrocarbons at a two parts per million, and benzene, a known carcinogen, at less than one part per billion. Neither by federal standards poses a hazard for groundwater, or even to drinking water at those levels. But the reporter and the public will want to know, "Is it there or not?" How do you handle the answer?

The answer is, "Yes, it's there, but there are government standards that say there's no need for alarm given the levels we're finding."

Another approach is to say, "The problem isn't, 'Is it there or not?,' but rather, 'How risky is it if it's there?" That permits you to explain the degree or level of risk of the substance that's present in small quantities.

If you can avoid the "Is it there or not" dichotomy altogether, that's even better.

Would you let your family live there?

Reporters try to personalize stories so they provide information useful to the reader or viewer.

Suppose a story is about traces of a pesticide in flour. The traces may be well below the level allowed by government regulation, and pose no threat to the consumer. In the process of stating the facts to a reporter, the company spokesperson might be asked, "Would you let your family eat anything with this flour in it?" That's the sort of question that brings a story down to earth, where the answer will be particularly relevant. If you believe the data you've been discussing, then your answer would have to be, "Yes, I certainly would, and we do consume it."

The author has been asked when discussing pipeline safety, "Would you let your family live next to one of your company's pipelines?" My honest answer to that would have to be, "I would not want my family to live next to an oil pipeline because they sometimes leak." But then, I live in a home that is connected to a natural gas distribution system, as most of us are. There's really very little risk in that, and there's really very little risk in living next to an oil pipeline. Pipelines leak, yes—but not often enough for me to be overly concerned." Still, I'm less likely to be apprehensive about a small natural gas pipeline out in my yard or hooked up to my house than I would be about a 40-inch petroleum pipeline moving millions of gallons of gasoline and distillates through my yard every day. If that big pipeline ruptured, I'd be knee-deep in gasoline and in big trouble.

Reporters are rewarded for negative coverage

There's a reason why reporters cover negative news. They get more recognition from their editors, they're more likely to win awards and they are more likely to get salary increases for covering negative than positive news.

A reporter isn't going to get a raise or a promotion for writing a story about the great contributions a local industry makes to the economy. But a story that is about corruption in local government is likely to be featured on the front page, get noticed, and perhaps win the reporter job security, promotion and pay increases.

Reporters seldom wake up in the morning, look in the mirror and say, "Gee, I wonder who I can write something nice about today?" That's just not in the nature of the job. But they do sometimes wake up, look in the mirror and wonder "Who can I nail today?"

Sometimes positive health news will be covered

Positive information about health has a strong likelihood of being covered by the media, especially if a large number of victims are affected by a disease about to be conquered.

Take the matter of cancer. That's a disease that everybody loves to hate. Who hasn't been affected by someone in the family falling victim to the disease?

Now suppose that a new miracle substance is found that halts or kills cancer. That's a positive story, and it's likely to get substantial coverage. Example: researchers recently isolated a substance in green tea that is believed to retard cancer. The substance interferes with an enzyme that cancer cells need to grow. The discovery of that substance got widespread media play. And would you believe it? The positive publicity for green tea resulted in an increase in sales!

Negative statements get more coverage than positive statements

We've already covered the reporter's desire to provide "balanced" coverage, or coverage of both sides of an issue. While reporters seek balance, they seldom give equal amounts of space or time to both sides of an issue. Reporters consider a story balanced if both sides are quoted. They don't think they have to give equal space or time to both sides for that to be true.

When someone makes a negative statement, that statement is likely to get more time or space than a positive statement. In other words, the neighborhood resident who expresses concern about the siting of a hazardous facility is likely to get more space or time in the coverage than a neighbor who welcomes the facility. The person who thinks the water is contaminated by petroleum from an oil spill or who has lost income as a fisherman is likely to get more time or space than the person who says she's not worried about the spill.

In one recent study of print stories about environmental issues, negative statements constituted 58 percent of the coverage, positive statements received 18 percent of the coverage and 24 percent of the coverage was neutral.

Reporters don't consider stories where statements critical of an organization or situation get more coverage than statements in defense to be biased. So long as both sides of the issue get covered, the story is "balanced." If the negative viewpoint gets 80 percent of the coverage, that's fine. After all, if someone wasn't making charges or allegations, there wouldn't be a story!

On this subject, it's worth noting that reporters often favor negative to positive words. They'd rather call the facility a "dump" than a "sanitation facility." Organizations are great at dreaming up euphemisms for unpopular concepts. Reporters prefer to call 'em the way the see 'em.

What's a euphemism? It's a way of saying something in a way that arouses less emotion, a way that has less subjective connotation. When an oil pipeline's aerial patrol plane had to make an emergency landing in a populated area, the pilot's boss, put out a bulletin to all employees framing the landing as due to "fuel starvation." That was a euphemism for the fact the pilot forgot to fuel the plane and ran out of gas.

Reporters cover involved individuals, not uninvolved experts

Reporters are much more likely to quote people involved in an event than to seek out uninvolved experts for guidance on the extent of risk. While an academic somewhere in the nation may be the undisputed expert on a given risk, a reporter is unlikely to seek that expert out unless the expert is in some way directly involved in the incident the reporter is covering.

Chronic risk will get covered if it's on the media agenda

People who work in the news departments of the mass media have an agenda that tells them what stories are important. Unless a story is on the agenda, it's unlikely to excite a reporter into covering it.

Who sets the agenda? It varies from locality to locality. At the national level, certain bellwether media decide what stories are worth covering. The agenda-setters include the Associated Press, Cable News Network, the news departments of ABC, NBC, FOX and CBS, the *New York Times*, the *Wall Street Journal*, *USA Today*, the *Washington Post*, the *Los Angeles Times* and perhaps CNBC and the MSNBC network. On any given day, influential media in localities where crises are occurring may also play a role in setting the national agenda.

The local media agenda is likely set by gatekeepers who monitor key national media—the editorial review board of the local newspaper, the assignment editors at tv stations, the newswriters at major radio stations. In localities where there is a city news bureau, that too may play a role in setting the local agenda.

Chronic risk—the risk of getting cancer from slow exposure for many years to small amounts of a substance in the air, for example—is more likely to be covered by local media if the story is already on the national or local agenda. It generally takes some pretty strong persuasion or pitching to get a reporter interested in chronic risk.

One way to encourage interest in chronic risk that's not on

the agenda would be to provoke controversy, perhaps between two local authorities. The media just might get interested in covering the risk in the process of covering the controversy. Of even greater value is the staging of pseudo-events. While the issue of smoking and cancer may not be on the daily news agenda, staging a "smokeout" in which a few local notables quit smoking may generate news coverage.

Reporters are more likely to cover politicians than scientists

If a story about an environmental event takes on political over-tones, it's usually because the reporter's hunger for factual in-formation has not been satisfied. In such a situation, the re-porter may resort to calling politicians to fill the void.

When reporters are covering risk, they're almost ten times more likely to quote a government or political source than an academic or scientific source. Newsmakers from industry are quoted a fourth as much as government sources. The reporters tend to favor state as opposed to local or federal government sources when reporting people with viewpoints on the risk in a given situation.

Reporters cover involved individuals, not uninvolved experts

Reporters are much more likely to quote people involved in an event than to seek out uninvolved experts for guidance on the extent of risk. While an academic somewhere in the nation may be the undisputed expert on a given risk subject, a reporter is unlikely to seek that expert out—unless the expert is in some way directly involved in the incident the reporter is covering.

MINI-CASE: FED UP WITH AIRLINES, BUSINESS TRAVELERS FIGHT BACK

You are the public relations vice president of one of America's largest airlines. Your company faces a challenging situation if not a crisis. In a startling change of behavior, normally placid business travelers, fed up with escalating fares, deteriorating service, cramped seating, irritable ticket agents and on-board employees, overbooked flights and a host of other irritants have begun using technology to fight back.

The last thing your airline needs right now is to lose its most valuable passengers. The business travelers, who normally make up about 50 percent of your airline's traffic, account for a dispro-portionate 65 percent of carrier revenues.

After years of bottom-line growth in profits, your carrier's earn-ings first began to be threatened in 2000 by skyrocketing jet-fuel prices. Then, following a series of ill-timed and ill-advised interest rate increases by the Federal Reserve Board, the economy softened. Business travel declined as corporations tight-ened their belts. To make matters worse, labor discontent has resulted in wage and salary increases for employees at a time when these expenses needed to be kept in check. Caught be-tween the twin pressures of rising costs and falling revenue, America's airlines face a net loss of $2 to $2.5 billion in 2001, ending a profit streak that had lasted for six years.

Travelers are increasingly scouting for cheaper fares or stay-ing home. The first quarter of 2001 represented the biggest drop ever recorded in the percentage of full-price coach and first-class tickets—the tickets most likely to be bought by business travel-ers. Only seven percent of travelers are now paying full coach prices, down from 12 percent. First class travelers now consti-tute only one percent of ticket-buyers, down from two percent.

Among the ways the fed-up business travelers are fighting back are by:

• Bidding for cheaper tickets at on-line services such as Priceline.

• Comparison-shopping at online sites such as Travelocity.

• Taking flights that have one or two extra legs but save con-siderably on ticket price.

• Using corporate travel bureaus to scroll down lists of avail-able flights, and learning they can save hundreds of dollars by taking earlier or later flights.

Whew! Talk about ways an angry public can retaliate!

Discussion Questions

1. The president of the airline for which you work asks you in a cabinet meeting what public relations can do to reverse the

trend in which business travelers are fighting back. What is your answer?

2. What communication channels are available to you for use in influencing business travelers?

3. With the heads of what other departments would you want to coordinate before coming up with a program? What are your reasons for selecting these department heads?

Situation Continued. It's now September 12, 2001. Yesterday, four American airliners were hijacked. Two crashed into the twin towers of the World Trade Center in New York; one crashed into the Pentagon in Washington; and the fourth crashed in a field in Pennsylvania. None of them were yours, but all air traffic in the United States is grounded. The country has been attacked in an act of war and is retaliating by declaring war on all terrorists. What until now has merely been a most challenging situation is now a true crisis. Air traffic will almost certainly decline when flying resumes. A large part of the American population has become afraid to fly. Your airline is bleeding red ink. It will be necessary to lay off thousands of employees. It may be necessary to declare bankruptcy. An emergency meeting of the airline's officers has been called by the company president. You're preparing for that meeting.

Discussion Questions

1. What are the key publics with which you believe you will have to communicate on behalf of your employer?

2. What message channels will be the most important?

3. What five "must airs" will the airline spokespersons and messages most need to communicate?

NOTES

[1] Ron Fournier, Associated Press, "'Bushies excel at damage control," *Atlanta Journal-Constitution*, Feb. 9, 2001, p. A14.

CHAPTER SEVEN

Negotiating with Difficult People

We have all had encounters with someone else who simply "would not listen to reason." In a family, this difficult person might have been an angry child, an obnoxious relative or a quarrelsome spouse. In a work situation, the difficult person may have been your boss, a co-worker on a project team, an adversary in negotiations for a business deal or even a representative of organized labor who absolutely refused to listen to your arguments. Right now, you can probably think of a dozen people you regard as "difficult" when it comes to matters of persuasion, or "getting them to see things your way."

The term "difficult person" is used here to describe someone who wants something that is contrary to what you want. A child who is normally loving becomes "difficult" when you want her to clean her room and she wants to do something else. A fellow worker who is normally a cooperative team player becomes "difficult" when you want him to approve a project and he thinks the project is a bad idea.

THE DIFFICULT ADVERSARY MAY BE
ONE PERSON OR MANY

In negotiating theory, we tend to think of our adversary as a single person across the table. We want something, and that other person wants something else contrary to our interests.

When it comes to working with angry people and outraged publics, keep that word "publics" in mind. The skills that work in negotiating with a single individual across the table also work when the adversary is a number of hostile individuals at a public meeting.

In the "outraged publics" situation, you can use the techniques outlined in this chapter with each individual who rises up to speak out at the public meeting, angrily denouncing you or your cause.

As you read through the various hints and skills in this chapter, think not only of your opponent as that single individual across the table, but as a group of individuals at a public meeting, or as the viewers of the evening television news watching the coverage of a public meeting characterized by outrage.

WHY YOU SHOULD MASTER
NEGOTIATING SKILLS

If you are at all normal, you've already done a lot of negotiating in your life. If you have a teenager who wants to borrow the car for a date, you probably negotiate the time that car and the teenager are to be back home and how much gasoline is to be left in the car's tank. Perhaps you negotiate with another member of the family over who takes out the garbage, or whether the bathroom tissue should go with the paper toward or opposite the dispenser. We can all benefit from learning how to do better in these domestic negotiations.

In business, if you are responsible for accomplishing a specific task or mission, and expect that you will have to deal with a contrarian, it's even more important that you master basic negotiating skills.

Suppose, by way of example, that you work for a concrete company. State regulatory officials have decided to grant a permit to your company that will allow it to build a facility where hazardous waste will be incinerated as a fuel for concrete manufacture. The site is near a middle-class residential neighborhood. Resenting the state's interference in their local community, the residents are likely to rise in anger, putting together a fund to pay for litigation to stop your proposed facility, meanwhile collecting information on its safety. The legal process and the anger of the community both will encourage the public to overestimate the degree of risk posed by the facility. At this stage, an industry planning to build a controversial facility, with encouragement from state officials, usually offers a package of compensation, concessions and incentives that would leave the residents of the community better off financially and in a safer condition.

When confronted with the need to make a decision about such a package, residents of the local community will likely put control issues ahead of the financial benefits that might accrue to the community.

Now imagine that the community is told it has the power to cancel or veto the project altogether, or, as an alternative, to negotiate its own package with the industry. In such a case, the residents of the community are likely to form a committee and imaginatively negotiate a set of concessions with the industry. But such negotiating only becomes possible when the community residents feel they are indeed empowered to negotiate, and are not being forced into decisions by government and industry.

DECIDING WHAT YOU WANT

In a situation like the one just outlined, there are three outcomes you are likely to want from the community:
- Approval
- Acquiescence
- Action

Before a negotiation begins, you want to know which of these three outcomes you want. Do you want your adversaries to reverse their stance and approve of your project? Do you simply want the adversaries to shut up and stop opposing the project? Do you want the opponents to take an action such as putting their houses up for sale with you underwriting the fair value of the properties?

NEGOTIATE, MEDIATE, ARBITRATE— ALTERNATIVE DISPUTE RESOLUTION

Another important decision that needs to be made is the level of peacemaking that will be used. The term *alternative dispute resolution* is used to describe three different techniques that might be used to accomplish the same end:

- Negotiation
- Mediation
- Arbitration

Anyone can be a negotiator. You don't have to be a lawyer to negotiate purchase of a new car. Mediation and arbitration require special training. The mediator goes between adversaries and seeks a nonbinding solution to a dispute. The arbitrator's decisions are binding on the adversaries involved.

DuPont, the big chemical company, recently faced a difficult situation in Georgia, where the chemical giant wanted to open a titanium pit mine adjacent to the Okefenokee swamp, one of Georgia's natural wonders. Environmentalists and the *Atlanta Journal-Constitution* almost immediately raised concerns about the project.

One of DuPont's lawyers said that the company would form a council of leading environmentalists and local residents, and that if one member of the Council, after reviewing the company's proposal for the project, continued to object to it, DuPont would abandon the project. That put control solely in the hands of the publics most likely to oppose the project. On the surface, that sounded good. However, DuPont announced before long that its lawyer wasn't exactly right about what DuPont was willing to do, and the commitment was gracefully withdrawn.

Incorrect strategies for dealing with a difficult opponent almost always include:

- Striking back. You'll probably just provoke your opponent.
- Giving in. Your opponent will be encouraged to ask for more.

WHY PEOPLE RESIST NEGOTIATING

What makes an opponent difficult? Refuse to negotiate? Go on the attack in a negotiation situation?

Your opponent may still be using the conventional negotiating tactics he or she learned in the sandbox as a child—perhaps offering to share the toy you want, perhaps thwarting you by throwing sand, pitching a fit, crying, fighting and biting or whatever else works. More likely, your adversary in the dispute in more adult fashion:

- May see giving in as the only alternative—and doesn't want to do that.

- May not see how negotiation will benefit her or him.
- May feel he or she will lose face by backing down—even if negotiation would ultimately benefit him or her.
- May be feeling emotions such as fear or distrust.
- May be experiencing emotions such as anger and hostility.
- May be convinced that she or he is right, and that you are wrong, and not worth listening to.
- May be seeing the world as "eat or be eaten," and may feel justified in using nasty tactics.
- May reject negotiation solely because it's your idea instead of hers or his.
- May regard negotiation as a win-lose situation, in which case he or she plays only to win. In other words, your opponent's attitude may be, "What's mine is mine, but what's yours is negotiable."

YOU WANT TO
GET YOUR OPPONENT PAST "NO"

One of the first words children learn is "no!" That's important, because what you want to do in a negotiation with a difficult person is get that person past childishly thinking "no" into the more positive area where negotiation becomes possible.

Barriers you must overcome in order to get your opponent past "no" include:
- Negative emotions that block reason.
- Negotiating habits ingrained by time.
- Skepticism about the benefits that might accrue from an agreement.
- Your adversary's perception of his or her own power in the specific situation.
- Your own emotional reactions to the opponent.

DON'T REACT TO YOUR OPPONENT

Three common reactions most people have when confronted with unpleasant situation are:
- To strike back, "fight fire with fire," "give him a taste of his own medicine."

- To give in.
- To break off. If it's a marriage, get a divorce. If it's a job, resign.

Don't strike back. There are distinct dangers in striking back. Occasionally, you might show your opponent that "two can play the game," and the adversary will back off. More often, this strategy will get you into a futile and costly confrontation. One of the disadvantages of striking back is that escalation often follows—a shooting match, a corporate showdown, a lawsuit or a war. Your opponent may be very good at playing hardball, and may want you to attack. Another disadvantage is that striking back usually damages your long-term relationships. You may win the battle, but you'll probably lose the war.

In a recent situation at an oil pipeline company, the district leader of one of the company's four districts needed the support of six subordinate operations managers to implement a new system. Five of the operations managers supported the change, but one did not, and that one dissenter was very vocal about his feelings. What should the leader do? The leader threatened to take the matter to the company vice president to which he reported. That only enraged the dissenting operations manager. The leader then, at a Strategy Team meeting, took the matter to the company president. The CEO refused to intervene. The new system was never implemented.

Don't give in. Some of the disadvantages of giving in to your opponent include:

- You'll feel bad. That's often the case when a parent disciplines a child. The parent ends up feeling worse than the disciplined sibling.
- You'll reward your opponent for bad behavior. That can lead to the bad behavior being repeated each time there is another confrontation or dispute.
- You'll get a reputation for weakness that your opponent will exploit in future.
- You may reinforce your opponent's behavior. Giving in to a child's temper tantrum may encourage the child to repeat the behavior.
- Your opponent may come back for further concessions.

Don't break off. When our feelings are hurt and emotions run high, it's not uncommon to decide that the best course of action is to break off the relationship—to dissolve the partnership, get a divorce, take whatever other actions are necessary for the adversaries to go separate ways.

The disadvantages to breaking off include:

• The financial and emotional costs of dissolving the partnership may be high.

• We often come to regret hasty reactions.

• Decisions based purely on emotion are seldom good decisions. The best decisions we make are usually those based on intellect, not those that were based on runaway emotiosn. That's not to deny that there are certain powers of intuition on which we must rely when making decisions.

Distancing

Moreoften than not, it's wisest to avoid reacting at all to an adversary. In the process of reacting, we may lose sight of our best interests. Further, your opponent in many adversarial situations wants you to react. He or she may be trying to dangle a baited line before you in the hope that you, like a fish, will take the bait. That can give the opponent control over you. Finally, reaction may feed an unproductive cycle of action and reaction which goes on endlessly.

What should you do when emotions are running high in a confrontation? You should distance yourself from the emotion.

One technique you might employ is to imagine yourself as a dispassionate observer, a member of an audience watching a confrontation between actors on a stage. You might imagine yourself as a sort of "*deus ex machina*" who will descend at the right moment to resolve the conflict taking part on the stage. Or perhaps you may find it easier to picture yourself in your imagination on a back porch watching a quarrel between two neighbors, knowing that the two will eventually call on you to come over and resolve the conflict.

The trick is to distance yourself to where you can observe the negotiation dispassionately.

While dispassionately observing, keep your eyes on the prize. The prize in negotiating is not to beat your opponent, but to satisfy your interests. While you are rocking on the back porch as an observer, or sitting on a perch looking down on the action on stage, you need to be figuring out what your interests are.

Suppose that you want enough extra salary, over and above

your present pay, to buy a boat and remodel your house. Your position might be, "I want a 10 percent pay raise." While it may not be possible to obtain your goal, it is often possible to satisfy your interests. You might not get 10 percent, but you could get enough to buy the extras you want.

Fallback positions

It often happens that you can't satisfy your own interests unless you satisfy the interests of another party—your boss, your spouse, your child, your negotiation adversary.

When you must satisfy the interests of another party to satisfy your own, you probably won't get everything you want by negotiating for it. For that reason, it helps to have fallback positions for your main goal. These fallback positions should permit both you and your opponent to achieve your separate interests. In other words, the fallback positions set you up for a win-win situation with your adversary.

One of these fallback positions will be your only alternative to a negotiated solution—the action you will need to take to satisfy your interests if you cannot obtain a negotiated solution or agreement with your adversary. If it's a business situation, this worst case position might be to find a job with another firm. By all means, if you think you'll fall back to the worst case, start looking for that other job now. It's far easier to move from one position of employment to another than to move to a position of employment from a position of unemployment. If it's a family situation, the solution might be something from as simple to cleaning up a child's room yourself, to as extreme as getting a divorce.

Once you've identified the worst case fallback or alternative, you can decide if it's worth negotiating a compromise that only in part meets your interests.

If you decide negotiation best suits your needs, stay focussed on the goals you hope to achieve through the negotiation process.

Common ploys and tactics of adversaries

If your opponent takes a position aimed at denying your goals, identify the tactics your opponent is using. You can ward off an "evil demon" if you know its name. Many ploys, incidentally, will depend on you not realizing what's happening to you. Here are some of the more common tactics adversaries may use in conflict situations.

• *Stonewalling.* Being intractable, digging in and refusing to budge from a position. One form of stonewalling is the fait accompli tactic, claiming a situation is already "written in stone" and can't be reversed or modified. Another form can be found in the opponent who says there's "no way" to give you what you want. If your opponent is stonewalling, you need to figure out how to get around the stone wall. One way you might deal with this tactic is to ignore the wall. Perhaps a subordinate is refusing to accept responsibility for a project. You might ignore the resistance, and continue to talk as if the adversary has already agreed to take the project on. This can serve to test your opponent's resolve. Another tactic would be to reinterpret the stone wall as an aspiration. You might say, "I can certainly understand your reluctance to take on this project, because I know you want to do your usual outstanding job on the projects you're already executing, but I know you'll do the same excellent job on this additional responsibility." Finally, you might take the stone wall seriously, but test it. "I understand that you don't want to take on the entire project, but if we were to give you some shared responsibilities with another person, would that change your mind?"

• *Attacks.* Your opponent may threaten you with dire consequences if you don't accept his or her position. The opponent may attack your proposal, your credibility, your status. If your opponent is attacking, you might ignore the attack. That includes passive-aggressive attacks. Example: in an effort to unnerve vendors and get more favorable terms, a purchasing agent made it a practice to keep vendors waiting and to allow phone calls to interrupt meetings with the vendors. These are passive-aggressive behaviors, and can be unnerving. One vendor who had become accustomed to the tactics countered by bringing along a novel to read and ignored the buyer's ploys. Other tactics that can be effective in defusing an attacker include:

- Rephrasing an attack on you as an attack on the problem.
- Reframing a personal attack as friendly.
- Rephrasing from past wrongs to future remedies. (Avoid phrases like "You always..." and "Remember what you did..." Your

questions instead should be phrased, "What can we do in the future to prevent..." or "Perhaps we could keep the problem from recurring by changing..."

- Reframing from "you" and "me" to "we." For example, "How do 'we' (not 'you') stay on budget?'"

- Sitting side by side, not opposite. Remember the importance of body language? In adversarial situations, people tend to sit opposite one another. Facing is confrontational. Sitting side by side is less confrontational. That may help to in part explain why at a restaurant females prefer to sit side by side rather than across from their partners, while men having lunch prefer to sit opposite each other.

• *Duping.* Your opponent may try to trick you into giving in. "I can't give you a raise, but at least I can guarantee that you'll keep your job if you drop the crusade for higher pay."

• *Lying.* How do you recognize when an opponent is a liar? Any of a number of good books about body language will tell you that a liar usually can't control the anxiety that goes with lying. That will cause him or her to raise voice pitch and breathe faster. Lie detectors rely on this phenomenon to detect mendacity. There are other giveaways. A liar usually can't control the symmetry of facial expressions. The liar's smile, for example, may become crooked. Shifty eyes are another giveaway.

KNOW YOUR OWN "HOT BUTTONS" AND KEEP YOUR TEMPER

It's important that you know your own feelings and "hot buttons." Clues that tell you you're reacting to an opponent include the feeling that your stomach is constricted or "tied up in knots," your face flushing, palms sweating, heart pounding and other symptoms indicating an adrenaline rush. When you feel any combination of these symptoms, it's time for you to go for your observation seat on the back porch where you can watch the argument on the other side of the fence or to that chair out in the audience where you can watch the play on stage.

Some common hot buttons:
• Some of us react bitterly to criticism;
• Some of us can't stand being made fun of;
• Some of us can't stand to have our ideas rejected;

- Some of us can't stand being made to feel guilty;
- Some of us can't stand not being liked;
- Some of us don't want to make a scene;
- Some of us hate being called disorganized.

Expect verbal attacks from your opponent that are designed to make you angry and "lose your cool." If your opponent tries to press your hot buttons, don't respond in kind. Your opponent wants you to lose control so you can't negotiate effectively. Remember what you learned in the sandbox? "Sticks and stones may break my bones, but names will never hurt me."

Buying time to think

Once you have your own emotions in check, and are viewing the negotiation process dispassionately, take a breather. Buy a little time to think. Forestall taking immediate action

Here are some techniques you can use to slow the negotiation down and let emotions dissipate:

- Pause and say nothing. From your position on the back porch, let your emotions fade away. This borrowed time may also help your opponent to cool down. If nothing else, the pause will shift the onus for carrying on the conversation to your opponent.

- Let your opponent's emotions wash over you. Tell yourself it's doing your opponent good to vent.

- Be quick to hear, slow to speak, slow to act.

- Slow down the conversation by playing it back. Use phrases like "Let me make sure I understand what you're saying" to get your adversary to repeat points. Make sure you understand what the opponent is saying.

- Take a time out. Teachers do this with unruly children all the time. If you need more time to think, take a break. Meet with other members of the negotiating team if there's more than one player on your side. Call you boss. Tell a joke. Throw pictures on the table of your last trip to an exotic place to divert attention and reduce tension.

- Bring along a negotiating partner and spell one another.

- Don't make important decisions on the spot. Make your decisions from the detached seat out in the audience from which you're watching the action.

Remember: Don't get mad. Don't get even. Instead, decide to get what you want.

DISARMING YOUR OPPONENT

You can't reason with a person who's not receptive because he or she is feeling distrustful, angry or threatened.

To get negotiations going, you need to defuse hostile emotions. You have to get the opponent to listen to your point of view, and an angry, distrusting person is in a combative, not a listening mood.

The secret to disarming an opponent is surprise. Do the opposite of what the opponent expects. If the opponent is stonewalling, he or she expects you to apply pressure. If the opponent is attacking, he or she expects you to resist. Do the opposite. Listen to the opponent. Acknowledge the opponent's viewpoint. Agree wherever you can. If you want the opponent to listen to you, begin by listening to the opponent. If you want the opponent to acknowledge your point, acknowledge the opponent's point first. To get the opponent to agree with you, agree with the opponent wherever you can. It's amazing how such techniques can calm down an angry audience or outraged group.

It takes skill to listen to your opponent

Professional communicators know that effective communication begins with listening. In a conflict situation, listening to the other side can turn a stalemated negotiation around.

Listening requires patience and discipline. Instead of reacting immediately to what your opponent says, or plotting what you will say next instead of listening carefully to the opponent, it's critical that you learn to remain focused on what your counterpart is saying.

If your opponent is angry or upset, give a full hearing to his or her grievance. Don't interrupt—even if you feel your counterpart is wrong or is insulting you. Let the adversary know you're listening by maintaining eye contact, nodding occasionally, and responding with cue words such as "uh-huh's" and "I see's." When the opponent winds down, ask if there's anything more he or she would like to say.

Another important listening skill is to paraphrase and ask for corrections. Paraphrasing means summing up your understanding of what your opponent has said and repeating it back in your own words—but retaining the opponent's point of view.

You should acknowledge that you are listening and that you understand your opponent's viewpoint by using cue words. Use cues like "I can see how you view this thing" or "You have a point there." Other affirmative cue phrases that indicate you understand are "I know exactly what you mean" or "Now I understand what you're saying." You can even pre-empt your opponent—take the words out of his mouth—with phrases like "If I was in your shoes, I'd see it the same way you do."

Keep in mind that acknowledging your opponent's point of view doesn't mean you agree with it. You can agree without conceding. What you are really acknowledging in such a situation is your recognition of your opponent's feelings.

Keep in mind when your opponent attacks you or stonewalls, that anger lies behind attacks and that fear is usually behind stonewalling. If an angry employee says he just learned someone else makes $2,000 more for doing the same job, don't try to tell him why the other employee makes more. Acknowledge the person's feelings by saying something like "If I felt someone was taking advantage of me, I'd probably feel angry too." By acknowledging the feelings, you help to calm the upset employee down.

It's important when acknowledging to be sincere. The other person can usually tell if you're being sincere or insincere. If the other person feels you're being patronizing, the situation can quickly turn hostile.

In the process of acknowledging your opponent, it's important for you to project confidence in yourself. That tells your opponent that your acknowledgment of the other point of view is a sign of strength, not of weakness.

Building empathy with an adversary

Acknowledging the viewpoint of an adversary is one of many ways that you can disarm a hostile opponent. In addition to apologizing, you could:

• Apologize to your opponent if an apology is in order. If an apology is appropriate, it will frequently work to reduce anger or hostility felt by an adversary. All too often, we forget to apologize when we've inconvenienced or offended someone. It takes very little effort and is good manners to say "I'm sorry." We learned that in the sandbox, but tend to forget it as adults. Lawyers more than any other group today are guilty of fostering bad manners. They seem to feel an apology may be used in courts of law as evidence that someone in fact did something. The next time a lawyer tells you not to apologize for this reason, ask him or her to cite the cases where convictions or adverse findings were based on an apology.

• Agree with your counterpart. Another effective technique is to agree with your opponent wherever you can. As part of this technique, while it may be perceived as manipulative, you can set the stage for successful negotiating by getting in the habit of saying "yes" more often than "no." You need to get in the habit of saying "yes" as often as possible, and you need to get your opponent to say "yes" as often as possible as well.

• Imitate the body language and voice tone and inflection of your adversary. In interpersonal communication, more than 60 percent of the message is in the body language used by the communicators, more than 30 percent of the meaning is in the voice tone and inflection used by the communicators and only seven percent of the message is in the words exchanged. Once you realize the importance of body language and voice characteristics, and have become a student of them, you'll find that you can build rapport with an adversary by imitating that person's body language, voice tone and inflection.

• Recognize cognitive dissonance at work. Without getting too deeply into the theory of cognitive dissonance expounded by Leon Festinger, Elaine Walster and others, recognize that it is at work when you use the technique of acknowledging your opponent's viewpoint. Acknowledgment will produce cognitive dissonance in the adversary. That's because the opponent expects you to attack, and instead you compliment the adversary. That will make the adversary begin to wonder if in fact you should be friends rather than opponents.

• Acknowledge your opponent's authority and competence. At the simplest level, you can acknowledge the authority and competence of your adversary by saying "You're the boss" or "I respect your authority." If your opponent appears to be a person whose ego needs stroking, the opponent will usually respond to someone like you providing recognition. You can disarm the opponent by satisfying this need for recognition.

• Build a working relationship with potential adversaries.

People are more receptive to persuasion when their basic needs for food and drink have been satisfied. You might disarm an adversary by inviting him or her out for lunch, coffee or a cocktail. The best time to build a good foundation is before conflict arises, rather than waiting until the conflict is fully developed.

• Express your views without provoking your adversary. All to often in human communication, the person who strongly holds a particular viewpoint expresses it in such a way as to make a counterpart's disagreement even stronger.

• Stand up for yourself. Acknowledging your opponent's views and then expressing your own is more effective than either alone.

• Acknowledge your differences with optimism. Make it clear that even though your views may differ, you can still find mutually satisfactory compromises.

Provocative words to avoid

One word to avoid if you can when negotiating is "but." "But" is a word you use when you are about to disagree with something someone has just said. If you have trouble catching the "buts" in someone else's conversation, listen to a few of the radio programs of Dr. Laura Schlesinger. She's very good at hearing the "buts" in the conversation of her callers and at challenging them when they use the "but" word. You'll do more to establish rapport with an adversary if instead of "but" you say "yes...and."

Another thing to remember is to make "I"-statements, not "you"-statements. Your opponents will accept statements about you, but not judgmental statements you make about them, because they know you don't know about them and their viewpoints. Instead of saying to a child that "You failed to clean up your room again," say "I'm disappointed that your room is not clean."

Putting an "I" in front of "you" doesn't create an "I" statement." Bad example: "I don't think you have cleaned your room." Another bad example: "I think you broke your word." These are still accusatory statements.

Creating a favorable climate for negotiation

If you are going to negotiate successfully, it's important to set a climate that encourages successful communication. The right

climate can help you overcome the common hurdles to successful negotiation such as your opponent's suspicion and hostility,
his closed ears and his lack of respect.

If you've accepted the fact that successful communication
begins with listening, you're halfway home. It's hard for an adversary to be hostile toward someone who hears her out and
acknowledges her point of view.

Changing the rules

After setting a favorable climate, it's time to change the game.
You want to negotiate and compromise, but your opponent still
probably hopes to win without compromise. To change the game,
instead of rejecting what your opponent says, accept it and transform or reframe it into the negotiation you want to have.

This is a good time to use a problem-solving question or tactic that focuses attention of the interests of each side, the options for satisfying them and the standards of fairness for re-
solving differences. Following are some examples of tactics and
questions you might find helpful to get negotiation under way.

The "why" question. One type of problem-solving question asks
"why?" When your adversary tells you his or her position, ask
"Why do you want that?" "What is the problem?" "What are your
concerns?" As the opponents answer, they will begin to explain
their interests instead of their position.

If your questions sound confrontational, put them in indirect
form. Say, "I'm not sure I understand why you want that." "I hear
what you're saying. I'm sure there are good reasons for your
position. Would you tell me, please, what they are?'"

Remember when asking these questions that your body language and voice tone and inflection are as important as the words
in your question.

The "why not" question. Another helpful way to phrase questions is in the "why not?" format. Ask "Why not do it this way?"
"What would be wrong with this approach?" Since people who are
reluctant to reveal their personal concerns usually love to criti-
cize, you can use a variant of this technique to your advantage.
Bring the opponent's interests up yourself, stating them incorrectly, and let the opponent correct you. If that fails, tell him
your interests first, and ask him or her why not to settle the
matter your way.

The "what if" question. Another way to get your opponent discussing options is to ask a "what if" question. For example, ask something like "What if we were to stretch the project out so you weren't billed any more till next year's budget?" "What if we gave you half the raise you're asking for?"

Rephrasing. Another tactic that might open your opponent to compromise is to rephrase his or her position in a way that sounds a little different.

Asking advice. One of the most useful tactics for getting an opponent ready for compromise is to ask for his or her advice on how best to reach a satisfactory compromise. Ask for your opponent's advice on how to satisfactorily resolve the dilemma facing you both. A good question to ask would be, "What do you suggest that we do? What would you do if you were in my shoes?" This tactic is likely to flatter your opponent, making him or her more ready to compromise.

Fairness questions. Most people know the world is not always fair, but they want it to be. They want to be treated fairly, and they want to live in a system that is fair. Another way to open the floor to negotiating from fixed positions is to ask your adversary "What would make you feel that you've been treated fairly?" Or, you might ask something like "You must have good reasons for thinking that your position is a fair solution. I'd like to hear them."

Use open-ended questions. One of your goals in negotiation is to get your counterpart talking so you can determine the reasons behind his or her position. Closed-ended questions that can be answered with a monosyllabic "yes" or "no" might work fine for lawyers trying a case, but they don't lead to effective communication. Be sure to use a lot of open-ended questions to get your adversary talking.More hints for phrasing questions:

• A problem-solving question needs to be open-ended and eye-opening.

• Avoid questions that start with "is," "isn't," "can" or "can't"" They can usually be answered with a yes or no.

• Start open-ended question with words like "How," "why," "why not," "what" or "who."

Tapping the power of silence.

Radio disk jockeys have a profound fear of "dead air" or silence.

You are not a DJ. Remember during negotiating conversations that your opponent needs time to mull answers. Don't break the silence while he or she thinks.

Negotiating the rules

Once the stage is set for negotiation between opposing parties to begin, it's time to set the rules for the negotiation.

The rules may be very simple. "For the next 15 minutes, we're going to discuss the pros and cons of granting you a five percent raise versus a three percent raise. At the end, we'll agree upon a solution that makes both of us happy." Or, the rules may be very complex, down to the room where the negotiating session will be held, the hours of negotiation, the size of the table, who will have the chairs at the head of the table and so on.

Once the ground rules are set, you're ready to negotiate. Now you need to progress to a turning point where a satisfactory conclusion to the negotiation becomes possible.

MAKE IT EASY FOR YOUR OPPONENT TO SAY YES

Look on your opponent as someone who is serving up an opportunity to you—much as an opposing pitcher serves up an opportunity on each pitch to a batter. Some of the pitches will be worth swinging at, others will not.

Even after you have disarmed your opponent and engaged her or him in a problem-solving negotiation, you still have to bring him to a concrete agreement.

Some of the more common obstacles to agreement include:
• Your opponent may stall or offer resistance
• Your opponent may lack interest in your proposals.
• Vague statements may discourage your opponent.
• Delays may lead the opponent to lose interest.
• Your opponent or you may reneg on agreements made during the negotiation process.
• Your opponent may give a flat "no" to all your proposals.

There are four common reasons behind most adversary resistance to compromise. They are:
• The compromise is not his or her idea.
• The compromise may not allow for hidden agenda interests.

(For example, a bank CEO might be agreeable to the bank being acquired by another bank, but be apprehensive about the loss of his bank's name and identity as it is absorbed into the acquirer.)

• Fear of losing face.

• Fear of moving to conclusion too fast.

In order to get your adversary thinking along the lines of compromise, you may need to:

• Make a bully feel important.

• Actively involve him or her in devising a solution so that it becomes his or her idea, not yours.

• Satisfy the adversary's hidden agenda interests.

• Help the opponent to save face.

• Make the process of negotiating as easy as possible.

Involving your opponent

There are a number of tactics you can use to involve an adversary in the negotiation process.

Make your opponents feel it's their idea. Don't make the mistake of announcing that you have found the solution to a problem. Your opponents must feel that they have participated in the decision. Think of how many times management at your organization has announced a plan to streamline work processes only to have workers sabotage the plan because they were not involved in the decision-making process. Or, consider how often a government agency announces plans for an unpopular site such as a new waste disposal plant or landfill only to have the local neighborhood residents organize strident opposition because they were not part of the decision-making process.

Build on your adversaries' ideas. To minimize resistance, ask for and build on your opponents' ideas instead of telling them what to do. Take a lesson from the 17th-century pope who said of an abbot: "When the conversation began, he was always of my opinion, but when it ended, I was always of his."

Some of the phrases you might use to credit the ideas of your counterparts and thereby build rapport include:

• "Building on your idea, what if we…"

• "I got this idea from something you said at a recent meeting…"

• "As a follow-up to our discussion of this morning, it occurred to me that…"

Ask for constructive criticism. Another useful tactic for involving your opponents is to ask for constructive criticism. Incorporate suggestions from the adversary into your draft. An old trick every editor knows is to involve as many people as possible in clearing an organizational draft document. Each person who takes the time to make a change then regards the draft document as his or her own work, and will defend it.

Offer your opponents a choice. Begin by helping them to make small decisions. Start with the simple, such as "Is 10 o'clock Tuesday ok for our next meeting?" Give them a list of alternative solutions to choose from. Once they select an alternative, it becomes their idea. Remember the old Chinese proverb, "Tell me, I may listen. Teach me, I may remember. Involve me, I will do it."

Satisfy hidden agenda interests. Often, resistance to settlement of controversy stems from unmet interests of the adversary that you have overlooked. Identify the unmet needs and meet them.

Don't dismiss your opponent as irrational. Empathize with the adversary. Put yourself in your opponent's shoes, and ask, "Would I agree to this if I was him? Why or why not?" If you are negotiating with terrorists, demands for money may appear to be the goal of the group, but the unmet need of the terrorists for public recognition for their cause may be more important than money or other concessions. Remember to consider basic human needs, not just for money but for food, water, air, clothing, shelter, security, recognition and other objectives. And remember that people value recognition almost as much as they value money.

Don't assume a fixed pie. There are ways to make any pie bigger. Look, for example, for low-cost, high-benefit trades—such as a bottle of vodka or a dinner on the town in place of a raise. Perhaps you can use an "if-then" formula—"You want $15,000, but what if I offer you $10,000 now on the condition that you then increase sales by 20 percent to get another $10,000?"

Help your opponent to save face. Help him or her back away without backing down. John F. Kennedy in the early 1960s permitted Nikita Khrushchev to publicize the U.S. promise not to invade Cuba so that Khrushchev could tell the Soviet people he was withdrawing missiles because they had served the purpose of protecting the Cuban revolution. He also promised to withdraw U.S. missiles targeted at Russia from Turkey. To provide similar face-saving for your adversaries, you could:

• Show how circumstances have changed. Your opponent may originally have been right, but times could have changed.

• Ask for a third-party recommendation. A mediator, an independent expert, a boss, a friend can help the adversary save face.

• Point to a standard of fairness. If you're negotiating the price of a car, for example, and your counterpart objects to the price, show him or her newspaper prices for similar cars.

Help write your opponent's victory speech. Anticipate what your opponent's critics are likely to say, and arm the opponent with counterarguments. Help him or her to reframe a retreat or loss as an advance or victory. A labor leader seeking a 10 percent raise for the union membership could be offered four percent this year, and another three percent in each of the two years after that. A prospective bride whose fiance was reluctant to register a china pattern with the local department store won him over by letting him select the pattern. Give credit to the counterpart when making victory statements. Disraeli once told an ambitious citizen, "I can't give you a baronetcy, but you can tell your friends I offered you one and you refused."

Go slow. Break the negotiation into small steps. Pace your client. Stop to rest when necessary. Look back periodically to see how far you've come. By moving progressively from easier to more difficult issues, you can get your opponent in the habit of saying "yes." Start with a pilot project. Don't ask for a final commitment until the end. Some opponents won't take even the first step. If you encounter that in one of your negotiations, tell the adversary it is not necessary to make a decision until all the options are out. Don't rush to the finish.

MAKE IT HARD TO SAY NO

When the problem-solving game fails, people are tempted to fall back on the power game —for example, to file for divorce, to sue, to strike, to go to war. If you're on the verge of failing to negotiate a solution to a problem, it's time to try even harder for a compromise.

The power game is supposed to make your opponent back down and give in. But the adversary usually fights back. When you play the power game, you can easily end up with a lose-lose outcome. You win the battle, but lose the war.

Use your power to educate your adversary, not to defeat

The smart play when negotiations are faltering is for you to use your power to make it easier for the counterpart to say yes. Use your power to bring your opponent to the negotiating table, not to defeat him or her. You win when you seek mutual satisfaction rather than victory.

If the opponent refuses to come to terms, he probably thinks he can win. He may think his best alternative to negotiating a solution is out and out victory over you. In such a case, you need to convince the opponent that he is wrong.

Start by using your power to educate the opponent. One part of education is to let your adversary know the consequences of failing to reach a negotiated solution to the dilemma you face. You can begin this process by asking reality-testing questions— questions that will get him or her thinking of the consequences of not negotiating a solution. Some of the common reality-testing questions include:

• What do you think will happen if we don't agree?
• What do you think I will do?
• What will you do?

Be careful in this process to warn, but not to threaten. A warning is delivered with respect.

It's at this time that you want to demonstrate your best alternative to a negotiated solution.

• If the alternative is to go to court, perhaps involving a lawyer in the negotiations will begin moving you and the opponent toward compromise.

• One tactic you could employ at this time is to walk out of the negotiations, but you won't want to do this without careful forethought.

• You may choose at this time to let your opponent discover the alternative on his or her own. If you plan to get a divorce, perhaps it's time for the opponent to discover the preliminary papers. If you plan to have 300 minority shoppers tie up a department store that doesn't hire minorities, let the store know in advance.

• You may wish to actually take the alternative course of action as the negotiations break down—to go on strike, start the boycott, whatever.

• It may be your opponent who strikes first when the negotiations break down. In that case, you want to give consideration to neutralizing your opponent's attack without striking back. If, for example, disgruntled workers call in bomb threats, record the calls and play them back to the assembled workforce. When the Soviet Union tried to bring Berlin to its knees by cutting off motorized supply by road from the West, thereby blockading the capital, General Lucius D. Clay of the United States, rather than attacking the Soviet Union, countered by launching the Berlin Airlift, which brought needed supplies to the German capital by air.

• You may want to tap third-party force. Every negotiation takes place in a larger community. You might be able to enlist the sympathies of the larger community to thwart your opponent. Start by identifying potential allies. You might even consider appealing to the other side's constituency. In addition to mobilizing your allies and appealing to the allies of opponents, organize the people in the middle. You can use third parties to stop attacks and to promote negotiation. These third parties may be able to get your opponent to negotiate with you, or may act as mediators between you and your opponent.

• You may wish to keep sharpening the focus of the alternative to negotiation for your opponent. When using this tactic, remind your opponent he has a way out—that your goal is mutual satisfaction, not victory. A police negotiator has to remind a bank robber who has taken hostages that he does have something to lose if he kills hostages. Parents can remind a child who stole money that they still love him or her.

Let your opponent choose

Any of the tactics listed above will likely help your opponents choose between a negotiated solution and the best alternatives. Let them work out details rather than forcing them into an either/or position.

Even when you can win, it pays to negotiate

You want to forge a lasting agreement, not a false surrender or continuing hostilities.

Keep implementation in mind—design a solution that encourages your opponent to live up to his or her word. Geronimo might have accepted pacts forced on him while the horse soldiers were present, but as soon as the soldiers were gone, so was he. You want a pact that will be observed. J

Just in case your adversary has second thoughts about the agreement, be sure to build a dispute resolution procedure into the pact you make. Then, preserve a good working relationship with your opponent so he or she carries out the terms of the agreement.

Throughout the negotiation process, bear in mind that mutual satisfaction, not victory, is the goal of the intelligent negotiator. Remember the words of Abraham Lincoln: "Why, Madame, do I not destroy my enemies when I make them my friends?"

MINI-CASE:
NEGOTIATING WITH ANGRY INDIVIDUALS

Situation: You work for an oil pipeline that has had a spill. The spill occurred in a farm pasture and affected a single landowner's property. The problem is that 85,000 gallons of diesel fuel went straight into a sinkhole and the groundwater below. You don't know which way the groundwater is moving yet, and depending on which way it does move, the plume could affect up to several dozen families that live near the spill site dependent on wells for their water. Your environmental team is working to delineate the extent of the plume in the groundwater by digging monitoring wells. When it rains and the groundwater in the water table rises, you are able to pump large amounts of the product floating on top of the water out of the sinkhole and from recovery wells. So far, 35,000 gallons of the estimated 85,000 gallons that went into the groundwater have been recovered.

Background: Your pipeline is the responsible party for the accident. The accident was caused by an error of the employee operating the pipeline. He had closed a valve, then pressured up the line thinking the valve was open, which caused the line to blow out. Your pipeline has had a large number of accidents in the past, and is thoroughly familiar with the characteristics of the products it transports and sometimes releases into the environment. Material safety data sheets giving the characteristics of the product spilled this time indicate that diesel fuel does not contain nearly as many harmful ingredients as gasoline.

Gasoline contains far greater concentrations of benzenes, ethylenes, toluenes and xylenes, all of which are known carcinogens. At the turn of the century, it was common for "Doctor Mom" to dose the flu or a cold with a tablespoon of "coal oil" with some sugar in it. That didn't seem to do much harm to anyone, other than acting as a powerful purgative. While diesel is not particularly harmful, people in the spill zone who get their drinking and bathing water from wells have a right to be protected from the product you spilled. If you affect their water, you're legally liable.

Research: You know from having read the literature of outrage and anger that victims affected by an accident are more likely to respond favorably if they are given some control over their destinies by political figures and the responsible party.

Campaign objectives: Your objective in this sub-campaign targeted at accident victims is to minimize the amount of public outrage of the potential victims.

Planning: You prepare a detailed item by item plan for conducting small public meetings. The county executive wants the first of these meetings held on county government property. After that, you may hold them at places of your choice. You decide to hold the first meeting in court chambers at the county courthouse on a Saturday afternoon. The second meeting will be held in a room of a local barbecue restaurant; attendees get to eat lunch on your company before the meeting. After that, meetings of smaller groups will be held at your company's command post or at nearby motels.

Key publics: The key publics you identify are:

• Victims. These are the people in the neighborhood who might be affected by the spill migrating to their wells. You don't know yet exactly who that might be, but you have a pretty good idea.

• Political figures. The county executive is the top elected official in the county where you had the accident. She is well connected politically. Her sister is a Clinton Administration appointee with an important position in the FDIC. Your accident occurred in Tennessee. The vice president of the United States is from Tennessee—and the county exec is well connected with that power center.

• Emergency responders. The county has an Emergency Response Agency. Officials of this agency have been your allies. You recognize the need to keep them happy as your partners. They add credibility to your clean-up operation.

• Media. The mass media are covering your public meetings. You can't keep them out for two reasons. First of all, the county exec insists that they be permitted to cover the public meetings. Second, you know there will be a furor if you try to exclude them.

Key messages: You want to assure victims that your clean-up will continue until the environment has been restored. In the meantime, you will do all that is necessary to protect the public and to make the victims whole for any damages they may have suffered. You are already providing bottled water to anyone in the spill zone who wants it.

Key Media:

• *Uncontrolled mass media.* Your accident occurred in a bedroom county of Nashville, Tennessee. The accident is being covered by the local county media, which include a daily newspaper, a tv station and a radio station. The accident is also being covered, but not as heavily, by Nashville dailies and television.

• *Controlled mass media.* You've provided letters and fact sheets to people living in the spill neighborhood. You've also provided copies of prepared company literature—a four-color backgrounder resembling an annual report and other materials—to selected individuals.

• *Controlled interpersonal communication.* You control the messages and presentation graphics your presenters will use at public meetings.

• *Uncontrolled interpersonal communication.* The neighbors in the spill zone are talking to one another. You have individuals employed by the company, especially your right of way claims agents who are calling on people to make settlements, who can affect the rumor line. County emergency response officials can also influence the rumor line.

Communication and Action: Victims at the public meetings are emotional and make demands of the responsible party. A novice reporter with the local daily newspaper—who is terminated by the newspaper by the time of the third public meeting—violates professional ethics by attempting to stir up the attendees. Rather than covering the first two meetings, he attends and tries to provoke the audience into becoming outraged.

• At the first public meeting, an expert toxicologist the county exec has brought in from state government resources becomes the victim of the crowd's wrath. The crowd doesn't believe her reassurances. They expect state officials to be on their side. Insofar as you are concerned as the responsible party, an emotional woman who lives in a trailer near one of your recovery sites expresses concern about bathing her grandson in water that might be contaminated. Another victim, wearing a cowboy hat, wants to know if it is safe for the 30 or so head of his cattle he is running to drink well water from a well near the spill.

• At the second public meeting, the grandmother demands that an expensive water filtration unit be installed between her well and the trailer where she lives to assure that her water does not contain diesel fuel. The cowboy who lives next to her demands a similar unit to protect his cattle. There is not one shred of evidence that the wells of either of these individuals have been affected by the spill. The plume is still far away. Another angry attendee demands to know if property values are going to be adversely affected by the spill. She wants a guarantee that if she and her husband try to sell their property, your company will provide them fair value if they can't get the appraised value on the open market.

• After the second public meeting, you divide and conquer. Knowing that the larger the crowd at a public meeting, the more likely it is that a few angry individuals will control the tone of the meeting, you now divide the crowd into small groups of a half-dozen or so meeting on alternate nights in a small hotel conference room. You can now work more on a one-to-one basis on the concerns of victims than you could in the group meeting situation. The anger and outrage dissipates.

Evaluation: Three months after the spill, anger and outrage have all but dissipated. Financial settlements and releases have been concluded with most of the affected individuals. The wealthy individual who owns the property where the spill occurred has filed a lawsuit using an outside attorney who has represented other landowners successfully against your company. He says he is not upset with your company or the accident, but is merely protecting himself from adverse financial cost if he decides to sell his property in the future and it is found to be contaminated. Mass media coverage is now favorable.

Discusssion Points:

1. What do you do about that reporter who is attempting to provoke the victims at the public meetings to outrage rather

than covering the public meetings? By the way, his father is the dean of the journalism school at the university located in the town. You should also know that the reporter is a burr under the saddle of the county exec who would like to see him gone.

2. What do you do about the demand made by the concerned grandmother for a water filtration unit? How about the cowboy? What about the lady who wants her property values guaranteed?

3. What would you have done differently at the public meetings to reduce outrage? What would you be doing behind the scenes in advance of each public meeting to reduce outrage?

4. Does it really help to reduce outrage to hold many meetings with small groups rather than a few meetings with large groups?

REVIEW QUESTIONS AND EXERCISES

1. You are a negotiator with the Chicago Police Department. A bank robber has killed a guard and taken two hostages. It's your job to persuade the robber to release the hostages and surrender. You need to script what you plan to say in the negotiations. What words will you use in each of the following tactical situations?

a. To begin the conversation?

b. To recast the demands of the hostage-taker into aspirations?

c. To reassure the hostage-taker?

d. To ask open-ended questions to better understand the demands of the hostage-taker?

e. To used markers to indicate understanding and build rapport?

f. To meet a specific demand of the robber to talk to a reporter?

g. To build a bridge for the hostage-taker to retreat across?

h. To bring him to his senses, not his knees?

2. Right of way agents from your company are seeking to negotiate settlements with some landowners affected by a chemical spill for which you are the responsible party. What are some of the reasons landowners affected by the spill might refuse to negotiate?

3. You have an angry employee who wants a salary increase. You want to keep the employee, who is threatening to resign. Review the five-step negotiating process you will follow to resolve the situation.

REFERENCES, RESOURCES AND SUGGESTIONS
FOR FURTHER READING

Karrass, Chester L. *Give and Take: The Complete Guide to Negotiating Strategies and Tactics.* New York: Thomas Y. Crowell, 1975.

McKay, Matthew, Martha Davis and Patrick Fanning. How To Communicate: The Ultimate Guide to Improving Your Personal and Professional Relationships. New York: MJF Books, 1983.

CHAPTER EIGHT

Working with Outraged Groups

It's common today for activist groups to create problems for other organizations—businesses, government agencies, even for nonprofit organizations. This chapter deals with techniques that may prove useful to you when you're working with groups that have become upset with your organization.

Suppose you're a business seeking to site a medical waste incinerator in a neighborhood. A neighborhood association is likely to rise in opposition. "Not in my back yard" or "NIMBY" becomes the group's action cry. Or, the call to action might be BANANA — "Build absolutely nothing anywhere near anyone."

If you're a government agency responsible for protecting the public, you may quickly be embroiled in the action. If you're an environmental nonprofit group, you may be called upon to be an ally to one side or the other.

Suppose your organization has been embroiled in a controversy. What communications techniques will help you cope with the situation?

DON'T CALL THE PUBLIC'S FEARS IRRATIONAL

People who are familiar with statistics showing the degree of risk involved in a situation have a tendency to quote mortality statistics and expert assessments, expecting the public to agree with them that risk is low. The public usually has other concerns than mortality statistics, and is not likely to be persuaded by such statistics. In fact, the statistics may only serve to further outrage the opposition.

Let's say that you want to locate a halfway house for recovering drug addicts in a residential neighborhood.

Many of the people who already live in the neighborhood are likely to be substance abusers themselves, perhaps with worse records than the reformed addicts you propose to locate in the neighborhood. For example, about a fourth of the adults probably smoke cigarettes which contain nicotine, a substance more addictive than cocaine. Many will be consumers of alcohol, another frequently abused substance. A fair percentage were probably exposed to marijuana in college, and may still be occasional users. Don't be surprised if there are a few heroin or cocaine users locally. Some local residents may have prescription drug habits. Finally, most will be regular churchgoers who have been taught to be tolerant. Do you think you'll have any trouble locating the halfway house in this tolerant neighborhood of substance abusers? Hell-o-o-o! You better believe that, to the contrary, it's not going to be easy!

THE CORRELATES OF RISK

Risk perception experts such as Dr. Peter Sandman, psychologists Paul Slovic, Sarah Lichtenstein and Baruch Fischhoff, and a host of other academics have studied how people interpret risk. They have identified at least 36 correlates of risk that go into public perceptions.

Among the more powerful predictors of whether or not the public will view a situation as risky are the following:

Less Risky	**More Risky**
Voluntary	Involuntary
Familiar	Unfamiliar
Controllable	Uncontrollable
Controlled by self	Controlled by others
Fair	Unfair
Not memorable	Memorable
Not dread	Dread
Chronic	Acute
Diffuse in time and space	Focused in time and space

Not fatal	Fatal
Immediate	Delayed
Natural	Artificial
Individual mitigation possible	Individual mitigation impossible
Detectable	Undetectable

These variables can be clustered into three groups of concerns, but for now, let's consider them to be individual correlates.

Sandman uses the examples of radon in New Jersey basements vs. dioxin found in a New Jersey landfill as examples of how the public uses the above dimensions to determine risk. There's enough radon seeping into basements in New Jersey to cause a one in 100 lifetime risk of lung cancer. Although there is a high degree of risk involved in radon gas, the public isn't much concerned about it. The risk of residents in three New Jersey communities near the dioxin-containing dump getting cancer from trace amounts of dioxin, on the other hand, is almost nil. But people living in those three communities near the dump (Montclair, Glen Ridge and West Orange) became outraged at the discovery of the dioxin. They demanded that local government spend hundreds of thousands of dollars cleaning up the landfill.

Why the disparity in the public view of the two risks?

HOW YOU SAY IT AFFECTS RISK JUDGMENTS

There is no neutral way to state risk. The words you use to convey the risk will either alarm or reassure people in different degrees. The verbal cues you use—the way you frame or state the risk— will have an effect on the way people perceive that risk.

For example, doctors who are told a drug will cure 30 percent of their patients are far more likely to prescribe that drug than if they are told the drug will have no effect on 70 percent of their patients. A petroleum spill of 17,000 gallons sounds bad, but a spill "that can be cleaned up with two tanker truck loads" doesn't sound nearly as threatening. The way you frame the risk statement has a lot to do with the way the risk is perceived.

MORALITY ENTERS
INTO RISK JUDGMENTS

We all have ideas about what is right and what is wrong. Call it our conscience, our moral compass, our social conditioning or whatever—we all have attitudes, opinions, beliefs and values that determine our sense of what is acceptable behavior and what is not.

Most people in American society, perhaps conditioned by highly publicized events such as the Three Mile Island nuclear emission accident, the Love's Canal landfill pollution incident and the *Exxon Valdez* oil spill have reached the consensus that pollution is morally wrong.

When society recognizes that something is immoral, arguments about cost become irrelevant. It may be cost-ineffective to clean up a small oil spill that nature would normally mitigate over time, but don't try to make an economic argument to an outraged public. It would be like arguing police departments should not waste resources on catching child molesters because it's far more cost-effective to catch traffic offenders.

The public expects corporations to make decisions on economic or cost-benefit bases. Government agencies must frequently choose between regulating on the basis of cost-benefit or on the grounds of good vs. evil.

If the public has decided that something is morally wrong, and the regulatory agency decides to regulate based on a cost-benefit basis, dissonance may be introduced and the result may be an outraged public. Such was the case recently when the Office of Pipeline Safety, which regulates oil and natural gas pipeline safety, decided to regulate pipelines on a cost-benefit and risk management special project basis. Environmental groups, convinced that the OPS had committed sacrilege on sacred ground, went to the President to express their moral outrage. Fortunately, the agency was able to hold its ground and the environmentalists moved on to other issues, at least until the next big oil pipeline spill or natural gas pipeline accident.

Related to morality arguments are arguments based on the cost of human life.

When a value is placed on a human life—in the case of the ValuJet airliner accident in the Everglades, where it was revealed that the Federal Aviation Administration placed a value of $2 million on each human life lost in an airliner accident for cost-benefit analysis purposes—humanists will quickly ask how a cash value can be placed on a human life.

In the "social justice" arena, where moralists argue that undesirable industrial facilities are most often placed in low-income areas where the population has little political clout to oppose the sitings, moralists may note that "producing the greatest good for the greatest number of people" is frequently used as an excuse for oppressing minorities. As Sandman points out, it may be "efficient to dump every environmental indignity on the same already degraded community, but it is not fair."

PERCEPTION OF RISK IS AFFECTED
BY SOCIAL CONTEXT

If the public likes or dislikes an institution, that will affect the amount of risk the public will tolerate from the institution. If the public trusts or distrusts an agency, that will determine the degree it will believe pronouncements about risk from that agency. The degree to which our friends and neighbors find a given risk to be tolerable or intolerable will affect our own perceptions.

Factors like the above are not part of mortality statistics, but certainly affect how we feel about specific risks.

OUTRAGED PUBLICS, LIKE THE MEDIA,
POLARIZE RISK

The public generally sees the risk in a situation as frightening or as trivial. If the public sees the risk as frightening, then fear, anger, panic or paralysis may result. If the risk is seen as trivial, apathy will result.

The correlates of risk again come into play in such dichotomizations. If the public decides the risk is frightening, it may still agree to tolerate it. But if a business or government agency presumes to tell the public it should not be frightened, that may lead to outrage. When someone else makes the decisions about risk, and we have to tolerate the risk, the situation becomes intolerable.

THE ROLES OF TRUST AND CREDIBILITY

Two of the most important qualities in communication are trust and credibility. If employees are to be receptive to messages from management, for example, it is important that the employees trust the source of the message, and believe messages from that source. Trust and credibility are similarly important in communication of risk.

In these days of downsizing and reengineering, few employees trust or believe messages from management. T.J. and Sandar Larkin make that abundantly clear in their excellent book *Communicating Change*. Similarly, few people today trust industry or government to protect them from environmental risk. This is true not only of the passive, apathetic masses, but of the small, vocal, activist minority at the forefront of the environmental movement. Both the passive majority and the activist minority are suspect of all "I'm here to help" pronouncements from industry and government.

PEOPLE WHO FEEL DISEMPOWERED
RESIST CHANGE

If people feel disenfranchised—if they feel an irreversible decision has already been made without their input and approval—they may still decide to dig in their heels and resist. That 's one of the common ways that protests get started.

All too often in decisions made with industry and government in collaboration, the affected public subjected to risk or annoyance feels the decision was forced involuntarily and unfairly on it. In such cases, the public will likely be unbending in its opposition.

Risks where individual control is involved—smoking, fat in the diet, too little exercise, driving without seatbelts—will generally be tolerated by the public even though considerable risk to individual health and safety is involved. Situations where far less risk is involved—the siting of a medical waste facility, chemical contamination from a garbage dump, construction permits for a strip shopping mall in an expensive subdivision—are likely on the other hand to trigger active opposition because of perceptions that decisions are being unfairly forced on people.

THE FOUR MOTIVATORS OF LEARNING—
AND HOW TO USE THEM

An organization—business, government, nonprofit—that wants an audience to learn and thus be persuaded to a point of view, must realize that almost all learning is contingent on four motivators:

1. We're curious.

2. We're committed to a point of view and are looking for arguments to back us up.

3. We have to make a decision and are looking for information to guide us, or

4. We think the learning will somehow enrich us financially or socially.

Most information-seeking and most learning goes on because of these motivators. If you want to persuade, you must get your audience to attend to your persuasive messages. These are the motivators that get the audience to pay attention.

When the individuals in a community are offered information about a controversial subject such as the siting of a hazardous waste incinerator in the neighborhood, none of the four motivators is likely to be very effective. A few people may read the information out of curiosity. A little technical data in the information will be enough disincentive to stop the few with the ambition to read the material. Activists, on the other hand, will scour the information looking for support for their positions or evidence that their positions are not being considered. The general public, aside from those directly affected, will for the most part be disinterested. Why bother with technical information about something over which you have no control and that doesn't involve you directly anyway?

EXPLAINING RISK INFORMATION IS POSSIBLE

When people have motivation to learn, they will learn. That's why students who can't understand Macbeth in a high school English course have no difficulty reading the instructions on how to advance the timing on their cars.

Part of the answer is to reduce the technical jargon in communication. Much of it is not necessary. Studies of communication in the Three Mile Island accident show that technicians familiar with nuclear power communicated more clearly when they were talking to one another than when they were talking to the public in news conferences. The experts were hiding behind technical jargon in the news conferences.

The tendency of experts to mystify outsiders is widespread. It's not so much malevolent as a fact of life. Experts don't want outsiders to understand their trade. If anyone could understand what they did, why did they waste all that time getting an education and establishing their careers? That's why lawyers and engineers and other "experts" hide behind jargon.

In many risk communication situations, the public doesn't want to understand. The public doesn't want to understand because its members feel powerless and resentful. The experts don't really want to understand because they want to hold on to their information monopoly. The public likes to blame the experts for complicating the issues, and the experts like to charge that the public is dumb. If any real information passes from the experts to members of an outraged public, clarity probably won't be the issue. The hardheadedness of each side will likely be more at fault.

That's not to say that simplification and clarity are undesirable. It helps in even the most difficult situations. And when the experts really want to communicate, and the public really wants to learn, clarity helps a lot!

THREE RULES FOR SIMPLIFYING COMPLEX INFORMATION

How do you go about simplifying information? One way is to use more words, making the message longer. Another way is to leave out some of the information, making the message shorter. The experts almost never favor leaving out information. In fact, they usually would rather say nothing than leave out some of the information. Unfortunately for the experts, the public doesn't like long messages. It prefers to have its information shortened.

The three rules of thumb you may find helpful in deciding how to simplify and clarify are:

1. Tell people what you have determined they ought to know--the answers to their questions, the instructions for what to do

in a crisis. This requires that you think through your communication goals and your audience's information needs.

2. Add to the above information you think people will need to know in order to understand the information—the background and context they need to prevent confusion and misunderstanding. Try to figure out where your audience is going to derail, and give the audience the information it needs to keep that from happening.

3. Add enough qualifiers and structural guidelines to prepare people for what you are not telling them.

EXPLAINING THE RISK ITSELF

Part of the challenge in communicating risk is communicating the complexity and uncertainty of it. Part of the challenge is in getting around the public's oversimplification of risk into "It's either dangerous or it's not."

One way around such thinking is to show the benefits of the risk as opposed to the dangers. But this argument is not likely to be accepted by the public, especially

• If moral judgments are involved (it's wrong to put this in the neighborhood) or,

• If the victims are not involved in making the choices.

Another solution is the risk comparison—A is more dangerous than B, but not as dangerous as C. But bear in mind that risk is more than mortality statistics, and that comparing an involuntary risk such as a chemical emission to a voluntary risk such as smoking is not likely to excite the public. Comparing the risk of an oil spill to the risk of crossing the street may show that crossing the street is a lot more dangerous—but people are smart enough to know they only have to cross the street if they want to, and when they do, they can look both ways to protect themselves. The same people can't protect themselves as easily from a pipeline accident.

Another option is to provide the actual data on deaths, illnesses, or the probability of an event if you have the statistics. If you do this, be sure if it's appropriate to make a statement about the moral issues, about voluntariness and about the uncertainty in the numbers.

Graphs and charts are a big help when you present statistics.

People understand pictorial representations of probability better than quantitative statements. Ross Perot made that clear in the television messages he prepared for his Presidential campaign.

Don't expect too much from explanations of risk. People can understand risk tradeoffs, risk comparisons and risk probabilities. But usually people don't want to understand. They'll often resist the information, especially if they're outraged or powerless to change the course of events.

EMOTION IN RISK COMMUNICATION

Where government bureaucrats and business executives generally fall down in risk communication is in addressing the emotional needs of the public. Many have spent years learning to ignore their own emotions and those of others. As Sandman puts it, "Whether they are scientists interpreting data or managers setting policy, they are deeply committed to doing their jobs without emotion." In addition, scientists and bureaucrats have had to learn to ignore the individual, to recognize that good science and good policy must deal in averages and probabilities.

Thus the most common sources of risk information are people who are professionally inclined to ignore feelings.

How does the public respond when its feelings are ignored? They yell louder, cry harder, listen less—all of which plays to the media, and stiffens the resolve of the scientists and bureaucrats. The new resolve of the bureaucrats serves to further enrage the public. The inevitable result is a melodrama in which stereotypical "cold" scientists and bureaucrats do battle with "hot" hysterical citizens.

An important part of the answer is to deal with emotions first, and with substantive fact later. Acknowledge the emotion with statements such as, "I can tell you're angry about this." The acknowledging statement won't eliminate the anger, but it will reduce the need of the audience to insist on anger. That will free energy for people to focus on the issues. Legitimize the anger with statements like, "A lot of people would be angry about this" or "In your position I'd be angry about this too." Such statements make a lot more sense than pretending the anger doesn't exist, or worse, to demand that the anger disappear.

Statements like the ones just mentioned are part of routine

training given to police for use in crisis intervention, and in family counseling. Go to these sources for more information.

Remember also that while executives and bureaucrats may have spent lifetimes trying to eliminate emotion from their decisions, they nonetheless have feelings too. They consider themselves to be moral people, so it hurts when they're accused of "selling out community health" or equally vile things. They expected in their careers that if they were not rewarded with public gratitude, then at least the trust and respect of the community would be their due. What they get instead is community distrust, perhaps even hatred.

The same observations apply to executives who play a role in downsizing or reengineering corporations. They expect respect and gratitude, but get instead distrust and animosity.

What can result in such cases is a kind of icy paternalism, an "I'm going to help you even if you don't know what's good for you" attitude. That's likely to trigger even more distrust, and stronger displays of anger and fear.

Communication is more likely to succeed when both sides in a controversy recognize the emotions of their adversaries.

Sandman points out that emotions are not what is usually at the core of controversies. It's usually the issue of control that's at the center. It's control that affects how people define risk, and how people approach information about the issues. But, he says, the stereotypes of the icy expert vs. the hysterical citizen is valid: "The expert has most of the 'rational' resources—expertise, of course; stature; formal control of the ultimate decision. Neither a direct beneficiary nor a potential victim, the expert can afford to assess the situation coldly. Indeed, the expert dare not assess the situation in any other way. The concerned citizen, meanwhile, has mainly the resources of passion—genuine outrage; depth of commitment; willingness to endure personal sacrifice; community solidarity; informal political power. To generate the energy needed to stop the technical juggernaut, the citizen must assess the situation hotly."

THE BOTTOM LINE:
LET THE PUBLIC SHARE THE POWER

By now, you have hopefully been persuaded by the evidence that the best way to reduce public outrage in your favor is to let the public share in the decision-making power. People learn more of the facts, and more carefully evaluate what they've learned, when they exercise some real control over the nature of the final decision.

Sharing power is, unfortunately, not the easiest thing to do. There are a lot of legal, political, professional and even psychological reasons that make it so.

You may think that it's easier for government than for corporate officials to share power with the public, but that isn't necessarily the case. Corporations exist to make a profit. The corporation may well decide that the only way to make a given proposition profitable is to make concessions to the public. Government, on the other hand, exists to exercise power. How can government exercise power if it is instead giving up the decision-making power to an opposition faction? Answer that question, and you'll have an answer to the federal government's blunders at Ruby Ridge, Waco and elsewhere.

The resort of government officials when citizen opposition arises is almost always "public participation." What that means to the government representatives is a meeting where people are allowed to *ventilate* their objections. Government officials listen to the public venting, and then *endorse* the position they have already taken. Most officials have become thick-skinned, and expect a certain amount of public abuse in the meeting that precedes the decision that has already been made. In such a meeting, the government is likely to say, "We've thoroughly studied this situation, here's our foot-thick report, and here are our conclusions. Now we'd like you to have a voice in the decision. What do you think?" In such a situation, government officials are not likely to really listen to the public, and the public is usually jaded enough to realize that that is the fact. There is little power-sharing in such situations.

If you are proposing a project that involves risk for individuals or a community, the solution is to invite public participation at the start, and to continue to listen as the project progresses to completion. That means inviting public participation before the degree of risk has been determined, before decisions about completing the project have been made.

That subjects the organization to having to say, "We don't know the answer to that yet." But that's a better position in which to be than the position of having to explain why you haven't shared information you've had for years.

A list of options and alternatives—we can do A, or we can do B, or we can do C..." is likely to be more palatable to a neighborhood than "We've done our research and we're going to do A, would you like to talk about it?"

Sandman says that providing citizen input is not only sound policy, it is the moral right of the citizenry. That is partly because only the citizenry can explain what it is that frightens them about a given project. He goes on to say that then citizens participate in the decision-making, they're more likely to accept it for the following reasons:

• They have instituted changes that make it objectively more acceptable.

• They have got past the process issue of control and mastered the technical data on risk, and

• They have been heard and not excluded, and so can appreciate the legitimacy of the decision even if they continue to dislike the decision itself.

MINI-CASE: ENVIRONMENTAL JUSTICE

You are the public information officer for Delaware County, Pa.

Residents of Chester, a city in Delaware County, have filed a civil rights lawsuit alleging the state discriminated against them by concentrating the city's waste-processing sites in their predominately black neighborhood. The state has in fact granted permits for five waste treatment centers and transfer stations in the neighborhood since 1987. In Delaware County as a whole, there are eight commercial waste sites in predominantly black neighborhoods, and just three in predominantly white neighborhoods. The lawsuit contends that this violates equal protection laws of the 1964 Civil Rights Act, and it also cites a 1984 regulation that says any jurisdiction receiving Federal Environmental Protection Agency funds "shall not use criteria or methods of administering its program which have the effect of subjecting individuals to discrimination because of their race, color, national origin or sex."

A single census tract along the Delaware River, about a half-mile square and with a population of just over 550 people, is the home of five of the waste sites. One of the sites is a huge facility that burns trash six days a week. The air nearby is thick with the smell of burning. Smoke is frequently present. Dump and garbage trucks pass through the neighborhood in a steady procession damaging roads. Residents in the area complain of sore throats, headaches, itchy skin and asthma and say walking through the neighborhood involves a constant assault on the senses.

As one resident puts it, "We have become acceptable risks. We do not have the comfort of our homes, and... are tired of the noise, the smoke, the dirt and the trucks."

You are assigned to preparing a public relations plan for dealing with the situation. Discuss the actions you will take

Discussion points:

1. As you proceed to formulate your plan, what points will you consider under each of the following steps in the public relations process?
   a. Conduct research.
   b. Set campaign objectives.
   c. Plan.
   d. Identify key publics.
   e. Identify key media.
       (1) Uncontrolled mass media.
       (2) Controlled mass media.
       (3) Controlled interpersonal media.
       (4) Uncontrolled interpersonal media.
   f. Identify key messages.
   g. Communicate and act in the public interest.
   h. Evaluate results.
2. Where would you go to learn how others have handled environmental justice problems?

REVIEW QUESTIONS AND EXERCISES

1. Without looking at the list above, how many of the 14 main correlates of outrage can you remember?
2. We've said that people who feel disempowered resist change. If an organizational restructuring disempowers people rather

than empowering them, might this lead them to resist change? How might a restructuring where it is contended "employees are being empowered" be interpreted as one that in fact disempowers?

REFERENCES, RESOURCES
AND SUGGESTIONS FOR FURTHER READING:

Karass, Chester L. *Give and Take: The Complete Guide to Negotiating Strategies and Tactics.* New York: Thomas Y. Crowell, 1974.
McKay, Matthew, Martha Davis and Patrick Fanning. *How To Communicate: The Ultimate Guide To Improving Your Personal and Professional Relationships.* New York: MJF Books, 1983.

Colossal Pipeline

Colossal Pipeline was incorporated in Delaware in 1962. It's mission was to build and operate petroleum products pipelines. The founders of Colossal envisioned a massive pipeline system that would transport gasoline for cars, diesel fuel for trucks and locomotives and kerosene for jet airplanes to marketing terminals in the Southwest, Midwest and Southeast. The company's backbone was to be a trunkline system that originated in Houston, Texas, and terminated at New York City. This trunkline would be fed by feeder lines from world-scale Gulf Coast refineries that stretched from Corpus Christi, Texas, to Pascagoula, Mississippi and Moundville, Alabama. The pipelines from these Gulf Coast refineries would feed into a Colossal origin stations from Pasadena, Texas, in the Houston suburbs, to Moundville.

Colossal in the two years following its incorporation constructed a trunkline 36 inches in diameter from Houston, Texas, to Greensboro, North Carolina.; 32 inches in diameter from Greenboro to Baltimore; and 30 inches in diameter from there to the New York harbor. Branch or stub lines emanated from the Colossal trunkline to serve delivery terminal tankage at the major cities of the Southeast and Northeast.

At the time it was constructed, the Colossal system was touted as "the largest privately financed construction project ever attempted in America."

Colossal was the first construction project in America to use large-diameter, high-tensile strength steel for a high-volume pipeline. Colossal's founders were aware that 40-foot joints of such pipe had to be carefully loaded on rail cars at the steel mills where the pipe was manufactured or "rolled." If it wasn't loaded correctly for the journey to construction zones, the constant clacking of the rail car wheels over the cracks between rails could lead to fatigue in the steel—that is, to tiny hairline cracks that would enlarge a few microns each time the pipe was pressured up. Any 40-foot pipe joint containing such fatigue cracks could accurately be called a "ticking time bomb" that might fail catastrophically, with no warning, many years later.

Initial news releases issued by the company called Colossal "the yard-wide pipeline," a reference to the fact that the largest pipe in the system was 36 inches in diameter.

Colossal's stock was at its creation and is today still wholly owned by from eight to ten major oil companies—just about all of the integrated major petroleum companies except Exxon, Chevron and Shell. The owner companies put up $30 million of their own money and borrowed the rest of the $350 million needed for construction from banks and other private lenders.

The first leg of the Colossal pipeline, from Houston to Greensboro, was activated in 1963. The second leg, from Greensboro to Baltimore, was on line by early 1964.

Study Questions

1. Would local media likely be interested in the construction of Colossal?

2. Should the public relations staff at Colossal issue news releases about construction? Why or why not?

3. If you were handling public relations for Colossal, what would you emphasize in press releases about construction?

4. What sorts of pseudo-events would you stage to create media interest in Colossal?

THE "BLACK BAG" PAYOFF

In mid-1964, with the last major leg of the Colossal trunkline system from Baltimore into New York under construction, the executives running Colossal ran into trouble. A mayor in New

Jersey wanted a large contribution made to his political campaign in return for assuring that labor unions would cooperate with Colossal's construction crews. The right of way agent who received the request for what was clearly a bribe refused to pay it, but did relay the demand to Colossal's officers. In the absence of payment of the bribe, labor unions began picketing Colossal construction sites, truck drivers refused to deliver pipe to construction zones and Colossal construction to the New York Harbor, a critical terminus for the new line, ground to a stop.

The pipeline officers, fearing their careers would be adversely impacted if construction did not soon resume, made a bad decision. They paid the bribe, using one of their own to deliver it in a "black bag" payoff.

Unfortunately, the messenger sent by the officers, a high-ranking employee himself, fell into a Justice Department sting operation set up by Attorney General Robert Kennedy aimed at uncovering political corruption in the ranks of organized labor. In the ensuing months, several Colossal officers who knew the circumstances, in return for exemptions from prosecution, turned states' evidence. Because the government sting was aimed at catching dishonest politicians and labor union officials, rather than bribe-paying corporate executives, the judge who heard the case was more sympathetic to the executives than to the politician and labor officials. The Colossal president, who also turned states evidence, was indicted, fined and given a suspended sentence because he was viewed by the judge as an upstanding citizen in the community who'd had a temporary lapse in good judgement. The politician and labor union officials involved got prison sentences.

Study Questions

1. An experienced public relations professional from a major oil company had been assigned to running press relations at Colossal. Should he have been privy to the deliberations in which the officers decided to pay the bribe? If he had been privy, what should his counsel have been?

2. The public relations officer left Colossal and returned to his parent company in disgust. Should he have stayed at Colossal to get it through the bribe mess?

3. Public relations professionals must obey the law. But what

about moral and ethical considerations above and beyond that? Are there any mandatory ethical considerations that bind public relations professionals?

COLOSSAL IN RECENT TIME

Today, Colossal operates the nation's largest-volume refined petroleum products transportation system. The company is organized as a common carrier oil pipeline system, which means it transports petroleum products for anyone who requests service, so long as the customer meets the company's quality standards and other requirements written in the company's rules and regulations tariff. The company's stock is wholly owned by eight major oil companies, some of them original owners, some of them not. The $30 million investment of the original owners has been paid back many, many times over. These eight companies get no special treatment and pay the same rates for service as non-owner companies. They do, however, appoint all the members of Colossal's board of directors, and split among themselves in the neighborhood of $175 million per year in profits after taxes--the dividends on that original investment of $30 million.

Because it is a common carrier, the rates which Colossal can charge its customers—be they owner companies or other oil companies—are regulated by the Federal Energy Regulatory Commission (FERC). The safe operation of the Colossal system is overseen by the Office of Pipeline Safety (OPS) of the U.S. Department of Transportation's Research and Special Programs Administration (RSPA). Certain of Colossal's operations also receive oversight from the Occupational Safety and Health Administration (OSHA) and the Equal Employment Opportunity Commission (EEOC). When Colossal has an accident, the U.S. Coast Guard (USCG) or the Environmental Protection Agency (EPA) usually become involved in overseeing environmental clean-up.

Since original construction, the capacity of the Colossal system has been expanded from 792,000 barrels per day (bpd) to 2,148,000 bpd today. The company's original mainline has been partially looped with a second, larger, parallel mainline. This parallel line is 36 inches to 40 inches in diameter from Houston to Greensboro, and 36 inches in diameter from Greensboro to Baltimore. At Baltimore, this two trunklines telescope down to a single line 30 inches in diameter to Linden, New Jersey, and Staten Island, New York.

Over the years, Colossal has built more trunklines from the mainline system to provide delivery service to petroleum terminals in additional cities. The company's capital investment has expanded from the initial $330 million to $1.5 billion today. Depreciated value of the system is a little over $700 million.

In a recent fiscal year, Colossal had gross revenues of $670 million. Its net income after taxes was $159 million. Despite the fact that its rates are regulated by FERC, almost 25 cents out of every dollar Colossal took in accrued to the company's bottom line as profit. As in all past fiscal years, all the profit is paid out to the owner oil companies in the form of stock dividends. In the year just past.

While Colossal remains a financial success—there has never been a year since 1964 in which it did not report a substantial profit—the company has had a number of accidents which have led to severe problems with the U.S. Department of Justice, mass media, politicians, federal regulators and landowners who live on or near its pipelines.

THE TWO ACCIDENTS AT MINE RUN CREEK

In 1980, Colossal had a serious accident in Virginia. An inexperienced controller in training who was running a section of the pipeline from North Carolina to Maryland overpressured the mainline. The pipeline failed at the point where it crosses a lake which is the water supply source for Washington, D.C. suburbs, spilling diesel fuel into the reservoir. The company's newly created Emergency Response Team went to work to clean up the spilled product from the lake. The clean-up went well for two days, and the spilled fuel never endangered the water intakes on the reservoir.

Two days into the clean-up, a Colossal's patrol plane spotted petroleum on Mine Run Creek 50 miles to the south. This creek fed into a major Virginia river. It quickly became obvious to all involved that Colossal's mainline had broken not in one place, where cleanup crews were already at work, but in two places. For two days, petroleum from the second break had been flowing unchecked into the creek, and from the creek into the river.

The product had almost reached the intakes for the water treatment plant serving Fredericksburg, Virginia. Colossal notified
Fredericksburg city officials to close down the town's water intakes, and took responsibility for providing alternate water supplies. A crisis was narrowly averted.

The citizens of Fredericksburg were reasonable understanding of the fact that accidents happen, although Colossal had to
pay many damage claims to people such as businesses that had
to close because of water rationing. Mostly, the water shortage
inconvenienced people who were told to conserve water by not
taking baths and showers and to reduce the frequency of flushing commodes.

Then, in 1989, nine years later, Colossal's mainline failed
again on the banks of the same Mine Run Creek feeding into
the same river. This time the break occurred in winter weather.
Ice on the creek had to be continuously broken to permit recovery crews to vacuum up the oil trapped under the ice. A large
dam was constructed on the creek. That successfully contained
the product, and this time, it did not get to the river that was the
water supply for Fredericksburg. After two weeks, a little before
Christmas, most of the product trapped on the creek was pretty
well cleaned up. The clean-up operation was dramatically scaled
down, in part to allow employees to be with their families for the
Christmas holidays, but more importantly, to reduce the amount
of money being spent on the clean-up.

On New Year's Eve, with only a single contract employee on
duty to monitor the dam and recovery, a torrential rain fell in
the Mine Run Creek watershed. Rain melted snow and ice, the
creek rose, and although the dam did not wash out, rising water
flowed around both sides of it. Upstream, the rain washed free
petroleum out of the soil. By New Year's Day, the water intakes
at Fredericksburg had to be closed again because of a pipeline
accident.

One of Colossal's vice presidents argued against notifying the
city fathers that water contaminated with petroleum might once
again be moving toward the city's water intakes. The company
president overruled the advice and ordered emergency notifica-
tion, which took place.

On January 2, the city fathers of Fredericksburg demanded
that executives of Colossal appear at a Council meeting to explain dangers to public safety, what the company would do to

provide alternate water supplies and, above all, to explain why the city twice had to close its water plant because of a pipeline accident. A city attorney with political ambitions was openly critical of the company in media interviews that preceded the Council meeting.

Once again, one of the vice presidents advised against attending the meeting, but the company president prevailed.

All the major Washington media turned out to cover the Council meeting. Three television stations had news crews assigned to it. The Washington daily newspapers, plus local media from Fredericksburg, attended. The Fredericksburg paper the day of the meeting carried an editorial extremely critical of Colossal and its safety record. A front page story in the paper reported that Federal authorities thought the accident was due to rail fatigue cracking of the pipe. The 1980 accident had been due to rail fatigue as well. The two failed pipe joints were in fact very close together, perhaps brought to the construction zone on the same improperly loaded rail car. Colossal officials knew as they walked into the meeting the preliminary results of metallurgical analysis of the failed pipe. The metallurgical laboratory had already determined that the second failure, like the first, was due to transportation fatigue.

In the meeting, Colossal's president apologized for the accident and handled himself well. Colossal also presented its side of the accident to the media through on-camera interviews. The city attorney provided counter-interviews in which he was sharply critical of Colossal, and the reporters covering the event tended to be more sympathetic to the Fredericksburg city fathers than to Colossal.

Discussion Questions:

1. Should the city officials of Fredericksburg have been notified of the New Year's Eve dam overflow?

2. Should Colossal have sent its president and a public relations spokesperson to the City Council meeting on the evening of Jan. 2?

3. What sort of training or rehearsal should the company president have been provided before the Council meeting?

4. What handouts should public relations have prepared for the media covering the Council meeting?

5. What "must-airs" should public relations emphasize in media briefings before and after the Council meeting?

6. How should the matter of transportation fatigue be handled?

THE GREAT SPILL OF 1993

On March 27, 1993, Colossal's trunkline near Washington, D.C., ruptured in a hospital parking lot at Reston, Va., in Fairfax County, spilling 357,000 gallons of fuel oil. No one was injured, and there was no ignition of the product. Most of the fuel oil that escaped ran into storm drains in the hospital parking lot and in an adjacent parking lot belonging to the local telephone company. The storm drains emptied into an urban creek named Sugarland Run, which meanders for 10 miles from the site until it empties into the Potomac River. Immediately downstream from the Sugarland Run confluence at the Potomac are the water intakes for Fairfax County, Va., and Washington, D.C.

Almost immediately following the accident, news crews from Washington media and a vast array of Fairfax County emergency responders and equipment descended on the scene. A Unified Command involving Colossal and government agencies was quickly established in an empty conference room at the hospital in whose parking lot the accident occurred. While the county fire chief, who had martial law powers in Virginia, was nominally in charge of the Unified Command, in reality, command alternated between a representative of the U.S. Coast Guard and a representative of the Environmental Protection Agency. As the responsible party, Colossal marshalled its own employees and a vast array of contractors to contain and clean up the spilled fuel.

As product spread down the Potomac River, forcing the closing of one of the two water intakes that provide water to Fairfax County, a second Unified Command was established at an air base south of the Fairfax County Hospital that served as the main Unified Command. Fortunately, Fairfax County had another source of water than the Potomac, and it was not necessary to close the water intakes that served the District of Columbia.

Excavation and examination of the failed pipe indicated gouging of the pipe by heavy machinery, probably a backhoe. The damage occurred close to the point where a storm drain for the parking lot had been constructed over the pipeline some seven years before the pipe failed. Excavation of an adjacent pipeline indicated machinery damage that was not as severe under another storm drain. Colossal decided to go public with the information that it believed the pipeline failure was due to third-party excavation contractor damage. A National Transportation Safety Board spokesperson took exception with the finding, saying the damage could have occurred when the pipeline was constructed six years before the building of the parking lot. The official NTSB report issued a year after the accident said that while analysis indicated the pipe had failed due to "mechanical damage"—a euphemism for excavation damage—it was impossible to say which excavation or construction had caused the damage.

Meanwhile, politicians entered the fray. A local county commissioner with aspirations for higher office insisted that the restart of the repaired pipeline be delayed. A Congresswoman serving her first (and last) term insisted on an investigation by a Congressional subcommittee.

The planned restart of the pipeline was negotiated with the local politicians. Colossal compromised, agreeing to restart at a reduced pressure and to inspect the pipeline with smart tools before going back to normal operating pressure.

A Congressional subcommittee ultimately held a half-day hearing on the accident. The hearing was held after the Congresswoman staged a well covered news conference at the accident site. The hearing uncovered nothing that was not already known. Maritime opponents of pipelines turned out to distribute their literature to attendees and the media. The committee chairperson regarded the hearing as an embarrassment.

The emergency response phase of the operation was over in 10 days. By that time, the pipeline was repaired and back in operation under terms of the negotiated restart. Only rainbows remained to be mopped up on Sugarland Run.

As the emergency response phase of the operation drew to a close, the Environmental Protection Agency gave representatives of Colossal an ultimatum—write a Consent Order for EPA approval, or the EPA will write one for you. Part of the Consent Order was to be a long-term community relations and communications plan. 'If Colossal doesn't want to take responsibility for communicating with the local publics affected by the accident, the EPA will," an EPA representative warned.

Discussion Questions:

1. It's the first day of the accident. As the person in charge of media relations, what will your policies be for handling the Washington press corps and other reporters covering the accident? How often will you hold briefings? Where will you hold them?

2. Will you permit the media to attend Unified Command meetings so they can stay informed on the progress of the clean-up?

3. How will you handle the first press briefing? Who will make presentations? Will there be a formal news release?

4. By Day Two of the accident, media reporters are getting in the way of your field employees working on the cleanup, and have become a nuisance at the two Unified Command Posts and at your Incident Response Center. You decide to use a pool system to minimize the number of reporters going into the hot zones, and to control access to the command posts. How do you set up the pool? How do you handle access to the Command Posts?

5. The National Transportation Safety Board is usually cautious about making early judgments about causes of an accident. In this case, well before it has prepared and issued a formal report, an NTSB investigator pops off to the press and says you may have damaged the pipe when you installed it, and may be trying to divert attention from yourself by blaming someone else, the contractor who later built the parking lot and storm drains. How do you handle the resulting media coverage?

6. A local politician has demanded that you not restart the repaired pipeline until the community has guarantees that there are no other defects in it. What do you do—ignore the politician and restart the line, or negotiate a start-up?

7. A first-term congresswoman has decided to advance her political fortunes by investigating your misfortunes. How do you handle the subcommittee investigation she has demanded?

8. What are the essential components of your draft Community Relations and Public Education Plan for approval by the EPA?

THE PICNIC

Two and a half months have passed since the accident on Sugarland Run. Free product has pretty much been removed from the creek, although heavy rains occasionally wash rainbows out of the soil. You still have boom at strategic locations along the creek to mop up the sheens and rainbows that sometimes occur.

Your environmental people are conducting studies on how to remediate damage to the ecosystem over the next year or two.

As part of your community relations plan, you decide that this would be a good time for Colossal to host a barbecue picnic for residents impacted by the spill. There is a park on the creek that served as your staging area for response equipment during the spill. The park has a golf course, a driving range, tennis courts, a swimming pool, soccer fields and other recreational facilities. There is a shelter and picnic area with playground equipment for children in the park.

All told, some 10,000 people live in the Sugarland Run and Potomac River areas impacted by the spill. Some 250 families, about 1,000 people total, live in the immediate Sugarland Run area most heavily affected by the spill.

Discussion Questions:

1. How many people will you invite to the picnic?
2. Where will you hold it? What arrangements will you make for feeding people, for entertaining them, for informing them?
3. How do you get the word out about the picnic? Will you use mass media? Direct mail? Neighborhood leafleting?
4. Will the mass media be invited to attend the picnic? How will you invite them? What arrangements will you make for them? What if demonstrators turn up and the media decide to cover them instead of your love-feast?

THE PUBLIC INFORMATION PROGRAM

The picnic at Algonkian Park, although it was covered by all the major Washington and Fairfax County media, made only a small inroad into the need to keep the public informed about the progress of restoration.

Environmental teams from Colossal will be conducting a variety of studies. As the results become available, you need to communicate that to the people who live in the community.

People are worried about property values in the community. You must plan to reassure them that they won't have to worry about their homes declining in value.

Discussion Questions:

1. What role will face-to-face communication play in your efforts to inform the public?

2. What role will the mass media play in your information efforts?

3. How about controlled media? Will you use newsletters? Letters? Brochures?

4. What kind of surveying and polling will you do to track and evaluate your progress?

THE THREE ACCIDENTS IN GREENVILLE COUNTY

Colossal had three accidents in Greenville County, South Carolina, in the last quarter of the 20th century. The first two were on Mother's Day, 1979, and Father's Day, 1980.

The third occurred in the summer of 1996 and ultimately resulted in a federal investigation and lawsuits. Colossal entered a plea of guilty in federal court to a misdemeanor count on the criminal side, and was fined $7.5 million for the third accident. The related federal civil suit had not yet been concluded when this book was printed. If time permits, the instructor will discuss criminal cases in class

Printed in the United States
49829LVS00004B/43